DRIFT SMOKE

Environmental Arts and
Humanities Series

DRIFT SMOKE | LOSS AND RENEWAL
IN A LAND OF FIRE

David J. Strohmaier

UNIVERSITY OF NEVADA PRESS ▲▲ RENO & LAS VEGAS

Environmental Arts and Humanities Series
Series Editors: Scott Slovic and Michael Cohen
University of Nevada Press, Reno, Nevada 89557 USA
Copyright © 2005 by David J. Strohmaier
All rights reserved
Manufactured in the United States of America
Design by Omega Clay

Library of Congress Cataloging-in-Publication Data
Strohmaier, David J. (David Jon), 1965–
  Drift smoke : loss and renewal in a land of fire / David J. Strohmaier.
    p. cm.—(Environmental arts and humanities series)
  Includes bibliographical references and index.
  ISBN 0-87417-621-2 (hardcover : alk. paper)
  1. Wildfires—Prevention and control—West (U.S.) 2. Wildfires—
Environmental aspects—West (U.S.) 3. Fire ecology—West (U.S.)
4. Strohmaier, David J. (David Jon), 1965– 5. Wildfire fighters—
West (U.S.)
I. Title. II. Series.
  SD421.32.W47S77 2005
  634.9'618—dc22   2005011395

The paper used in this book meets the requirements of American National
Standard for Information Sciences—Permanence of Paper for Printed
Library Materials, ANSI Z.48-1984. Binding materials were
selected for strength and durability.

First Printing
14 13 12 11 10 09 08 07 06 05   5 4 3 2 1

For the "Unknowns"

CONTENTS

PREFACE

When I first accepted a high school friend's invitation to join the Crooked River Ranch Volunteer fire Department in central Oregon, I couldn't have envisioned that twenty-five years later I'd be writing about fire. At the time, in the early 1980s, volunteering to drag hose, squirt water, and throw dirt seemed like worthy public service, especially in a department populated by retirees in desperate need of young lungs and arthritis-free joints. Plus, getting to carry a pager and tear down gravel roads with red lights whirling and sirens screaming was pretty exciting for a teenager. For the most part, my experience with fire amounted to brief encounters with fully engulfed mobile homes and a smattering of wildfires in the sage- and juniper-blanketed high desert of a once-sprawling cattle ranch now sliced into ranchettes.

A few years later, while I was attending Central Oregon Community College, in Bend, as a wildlife biology major, another friend enticed me to join him as a seasonal firefighter with the Prineville District of the Bureau of Land Management (BLM). Though the job would last only a few months during the summer, the money looked good, as did the opportunity to work outside and get a foot in the door with a natural-resource management agency. For the next fifteen years, seasonal work as a firefighter with the BLM and U.S. Forest Service helped support my meandering academic path, which ranged from science to theology to philosophy to environmental studies. My knowledge of geography also expanded along a meandering route that followed smoke plumes and dusty two-track roads throughout central and eastern Oregon. Although the bulk of my experience as a wildland firefighter lay in the rain shadow of Oregon's Cascade Range, within the Deschutes and John Day River watersheds, opportunities sometimes arose to fight fires in other western states, such as California, Idaho, and Montana.

But regardless of where I encountered it, I began to see fire as not merely something to engage as public service or as a means to offset my ever-mounting student loans; fire had been present with me from my childhood—in the form of campfires and hearths, burning leaf piles of autumn, and candles associated with birthdays and religious ceremonies. In time, I also realized that for my colleagues and me, attraction to fire was not only personal—bordering on the spiritual—but also primordial. Whether confronting the wildfires of summer or telling stories around the rock-ringed fires of fishing and hunting camps, we were participating in experiences and rites shared by our ancestors. However, articulating the significance of this was, and remains, no easy task.

During the summer of 1994, before my final year at Yale Divinity School, I found myself fighting fire for the BLM in central Oregon, just as I had for the nine previous seasons. Unlike the preceding decade, though, this time the potentially deadly consequences of fire became real to me as fourteen firefighters—nine of whom were members of the U.S. Forest Service's Prineville Hotshots—perished on the slopes of Storm King Mountain in Colorado.

Another year in school passed, followed by another summer on firelines throughout the west. Then fall and winter. At last it was a time to write, a time to redeem fire from what I perceived as its too-often-demonized image, a time to celebrate fire for its role in our lives and society, a time to grapple with the deaths of colleagues who had performed the same work that I had and who would never perform that work again. These musings became the subject of my first book, *The Seasons of Fire: Reflections on Fire in the West.* But in the midst of celebrating the formative role that fire plays in all of our lives, a question lingered: Is there some unifying principle that might help explain our ambivalence toward fire on the landscape of North America, particularly the landscape of the American West? This question lay beneath my desire to study environmental writing at the University of Montana in Missoula, which, as I discovered, proved to be a strategic location for examining other fires that have shaped both fire policy and the collective psyche of land managers, firefighters, and the general public throughout the twentieth and into the twenty-first century.

More than a decade has elapsed since the hot, smoky summer of 1994 that catalyzed the reflections that evolved into first *Seasons* and now *Drift Smoke.* In the ensuing years, wildfires have garnered national attention for their effects on land and property, politicians have wielded the topic of fire as a means to inflame their constituents' passions and further their own careers, and firefighters have continued to lose their lives while attempting to suppress this age-old force of nature.

The discussion of our ability, or inability, to manage fire is often framed in terms of science. On this score, and understood charitably, the land-management policies of previous decades were often developed and implemented with the best of intentions, even if from a stance of incomplete and often erroneous ecological knowledge. Hence, our work today of restoring damaged ecosystems is frequently seen as a matter of rectifying the messes that our predecessors in the Forest Service, BLM, National Park Service, and other agencies created for us. The subtext of this story, though, is that today's science will show us the way.

This book challenges that assumption, arguing that not only is it important to better understand *how* the world works through the best available science, but it is equally, if not more, important to understand *why* we make the decisions that we do relative to land and relative to science. By examining a specific case, like fire, we might even discover how other aspects of nature—be they bears or wolves, or floods or disease—are affected by our values. And our understanding of loss, I've come to believe, plays a central role in the story of how we relate to nature.

While recent years have seen a proliferation of literary, historical, ecological, and policy treatments of wildland fire, the subject of loss relative to fire—in any sort of self-conscious way—

remains relatively foreign terrain. *Drift Smoke* is my attempt to navigate this terrain and illumine our relationship with fire as seen through the lens of loss.

I'm grateful to a host of friends and colleagues who have assisted with this project. My thanks to the Environmental Studies Program at the University of Montana, which granted me a B & B Dawson Award to conduct research at Storm King Mountain and Mann Gulch. Through the generosity of Ron and Nancy Erickson, I was able to research fire fatality sites throughout the northern Rockies. The archivists at the University of Montana and the U.S. Forest Service's Northern Region office were extremely helpful in tracking down documents and photos related to the 1910 fires in the Bitterroot Mountains and the 1949 Mann Gulch fire. I'd also like to thank Dave Turner, with the Helena National Forest, for his time and cooperation in responding to my frequent queries for Mann Gulch documents and information. Clint Dawson, with the Shoshone National Forest, provided invaluable access to materials related to the 1937 Blackwater fire. Finally, I'm grateful to Don Snow, Christopher Preston, and Jim Burchfield, whose textual cold trailing and incisive comments added greatly to the depth and quality of my reflections.

Behind each page of this book stand my co-workers with the Prineville District of the BLM (especially the Bakeoven and Grass Valley Guard Stations) and the Ochoco National Forest, and the residents of Sherman County, Oregon. They taught me much about loss, friendship, and engaging the fires of summer.

My thanks to Joanne O'Hare, director of the University of

Nevada Press, for expressing interest in this current project and for shepherding *Drift Smoke* through the always-daunting publishing labyrinth. And to Indiana University Press, my appreciation for granting permission to reprint "Threescore and Ten: Fire, Place, and Loss in the West," which appeared in the fall 2003 issue of the journal *Ethics & the Environment;* a modified version of that essay constitutes chapter 5 of this book.

Most importantly, I'm indebted to Gretchen, my soulmate, who, like many other firefighters' spouses, experienced the anguish that descended upon the West in July 1994. Her work with issues of death, dying, and grief counseling inspired me to explore—and continue to explore—environmental philosophy and fire policy from the standpoint of loss. She gave me a great deal of feedback on several versions of the manuscript, not all of which I wanted to hear, but all of which has made this a much better book than it otherwise might have been. My deepest gratitude to her for nurturing our new little ember, Ezra, who arrived during the final stages of writing *Drift Smoke.*

INTRODUCTION

We find a place for what we lose. Although we know that after such a loss the acute stage of mourning will subside, we also know that we shall remain inconsolable and will never find a substitute. No matter what may fill the gap, even if it be filled completely, it nevertheless remains something else.
—Sigmund Freud, *Letters of Sigmund Freud*

The American West is a storied landscape inscribed by loss: loss of species, loss of peoples, loss of cultures, loss of lands, loss of livelihoods, loss of hopes and dreams. This is an old story, at least as old as the late–Ice Age extinctions of megafauna some ten thousand years ago; it's a story still being written. For anyone who calls the West home, part of writing—that is living—this story involves remembering how these manifold losses have shaped the land upon which we live, who we are, and who we want to become. And smoldering under each of these losses is the story of fire.

Maybe it's so obvious as to seem trivial, but fire exists only because of loss. As an event in space and time, fire necessarily consumes life. Wood melts into charcoal and ashes; it also evaporates in radiant energy and drifting smoke. This is nothing new, for as long as lightning and cured tinder have commingled across the North American landscape, there has been fire. But there are other losses associated with fire, all very real, all very significant, too often ignored and forgotten. Fire in the West is a four-act story of loss—loss of fire from the landscape, loss of life, loss of livelihood, and loss of place.

Making sense of our lives and our world is seldom, if ever, a straightforward affair. Whether we're exploring new personal and intellectual pursuits or traversing a new piece of the landscape, we often rely on markers, established by others, to guide the way. Even today in lightly traveled regions of the American West, instead of well-beaten trails, there are routes simply marked with mounds of stone—cairns—along the general line of travel. In 1845 Stephen Meek led a wagon train on a near-disastrous journey through a waterless section of Oregon's high desert, all for the sake of a shortcut to the Willamette Valley. When the wagons traveled at night, scouts rode ahead and kindled fiery "cairns" of sage and juniper to mark the way.[1] Each act in this four-part story of loss is itself a fiery cairn, meant to mark a way through the grief and tragedy of fire and loss. However, unlike Meek's trail, these cairns needn't be traversed in order: where one starts depends on one's experience of fire. The markers are real and distinct and lead to the hope of consolation. But before any consolation is reached (if this is even possible), the cairns must be traversed, connected, even stoked under the ambiguity of a dark night sky. Unfortunately, these cairns have not always been recognized; when they have been, too often they've been viewed in isolation.

For the better part of the twentieth century and now into the twenty-first, an all-out war has been waged against fire. Fire has been perceived as a threat to forests (timber), homes, lives, wildlife, and natural beauty (Keep America Green!). With few exceptions, free-burning fire has not been viewed as a gift from Prometheus or the gods; on the contrary, fire smells of death, the hot breath of the devil himself. Framed theologically, "wildfire" is yet another curse of the Fall and, by inference, was set loose by Yahweh on the land after the cursing of the ground and the sprouting of thistles—thistles that got dry and then burned. We've shunned fire because it's an agent of death, yet we've failed to see that death can be an agent of new life. As the historian Nancy Langston has said, "We have never been very comfortable with anything that reminds us of mortality, but the death of its parts is what allows a forest to live."[2]

The old, almost entirely negative view of fire is changing. Many people are beginning to realize that fire has been, and should continue to be, a resident of the West. Indeed, the story of fire in the West is not without its happy endings, moments of beauty, comedy, and cathartic drama. Fire has played a positive role in ecosystems and cultures, and when fire is removed, genuine loss results—the first cairn of loss. Nevertheless, like the process of grief (that is, the process of understanding life), to truly understand fire requires an acknowledgment of all the losses surrounding fire: loss of fire from the landscape and loss of those things consumed by fire. As the pendulum of professional, even popular, opinion has swung from despising fire as a demonic evil to embracing it as a necessary ecosystem function, it's become all too easy to forget the ambivalent nature of fire, and the lives and values consumed in this seasonally recurring pyre. Hence, another task of mine will be to present an apologetic for grief—grief in a land that burns, grief in four acts in a land that burns. Let me explain.

As I traverse the second, third, and fourth cairns, I want to say to hell with the redeeming qualities of death. It's as if the ecological intelligentsia of land managers, activists, and academicians have become incrementally jaded to loss—deep, painful, and stinging loss. To lose something of value, something that we know and love and is a part of our lives, hurts. So it is between persons; so it is when fire levels a verdant landscape to charred rootwads and talcumlike ash. It needn't be board feet or personal possessions we're talking about. It could be any part of the land, even our identity, that is forever transfigured by fire. Before we sweep aside the so-called ecologically naïve or sentimental one who grieves the loss of a secret grove of pine or fir or juniper, maybe we should remind ourselves what it means to lose something.

I'm afraid that many of us handle loss in nature no better than we handle loss between persons—say, the death of a spouse. No sooner has one's partner been hermetically sealed and planted in the ground than well-meaning friends and family query each other about how the one left is "holding up." By "holding up" they mean is she keeping her composure? Getting along? Being strong? Okay?

But why should she?

Deep loss saturates one's soul, becoming part of one's story and identity, whether one realizes it or not. The closer one is to the epicenter of tragedy, the more difficult it is to glory dispassionately in the holistic beauty of nature, painted red in tooth, claw, flame, and firewhirl. We're an optimistic bunch, though, and we'll do everything possible to make the valley of the shadow of death nothing more than a fireweed-covered swale. Here I indict myself as much as anyone. Some of us have become ecological Pollyannas, joyously welcoming fire's reintroduction —the prodigal flame—to the very lands from which *we* exiled it. However, no matter how much we look on the bright side of fire, playing the "glad game" of ecological restoration and ecosystem management, the fact remains that fire has been and will continue to be inextricably intertwined with loss. Even when we admit that loss is a part of the human condition—at times even healthy—the pain and moral bewilderment that we feel following loss is real, and what is lost is surely worthy of mourning and grief.

Maybe for the long-term good of the land we need to let fires consume parts of nature, even parts we value or find beautiful. Most certainly, there is beauty in change: It's a wondrous process to behold a stand of lodgepole pine erupt into crown fire, then collapse into blackened hackles and a bed of ash that in time births a new forest. Nevertheless, we often, and understandably, try to extend the life expectancies of landscapes. Although we know that life will rise again out of moonscape charcoal, we also know that it may not grow to its prefire dimensions in our lifetime. If it does, it won't be the same. Taking a long-term perspective—"thinking like a mountain," to borrow the conservationist Aldo Leopold's phrase—may be ecologically and aesthetically desirable, but it's existentially difficult.

The psychologist J. William Worden identifies four "tasks" of mourning: (1) "accept the reality of the loss," (2) "work through to the pain of grief," (3) "adjust to an environment in which the deceased is missing," and (4) "emotionally relocate the deceased and move on with life."[3] These should not be viewed as linear steps, as if (in ecological language) they are seral stages of grief that will result in a climax community of inner harmony in which grief is fully resolved. According to the grief specialist Therese A. Rando, more likely they are "phases"—phases that possess no clear boundaries and that may be revisited more than once in one's life.[4] However, the very good work of grief and bereavement counselors, therapists, and researchers over the past few decades more often than not has focused on losses between humans. Deaths of animal companions, or pets, are the closest that many grief specialists come to exploring loss in the more-than-human world—this often being cited as an example of "disenfranchised grief," that is, "loss that cannot be openly acknowledged, socially validated, or publicly mourned."[5]

But while grief and mourning and consolation are most often linked to human death and loss, they needn't be exclusively. Any severed attachment requires the same tasks (phases) of mourning, as will our journey along the four cairns of loss associated with fire. All too often, for the ecologically "enlightened," grieving begins and ends with Worden's first task—"accept the reality of the loss." The acceptance of loss and its associated pain and grief are either treated like premodern superstitions or quickly exchanged for the rising phoenix of task four—moving on with life—as if no other tasks exist and as if moving on requires blocking out one's old life. At least partially, this attitude is the result of the metaphors we choose to interpret our world.

Much of life is matter of metaphor making, using familiar, commonplace images to organize the unfamiliar, the abstract, the cosmos. If the sole metaphor by which we interpret our world is death-rebirth, incommensurable loss is seldom recognized and the pain of loss is quickly anesthetized with the hope of renewal. I don't mean to imply that hope must be abandoned for utter despair; rather, metaphors in one situation may not work in another—birth may follow death, renewal may follow loss, but not always. It's that "not always" that I want to reckon with. As an event and a process, fire simultaneously is a chemical reaction, a motion, a happening that feeds off life, engenders new life, and affects all of our lives. Understanding fire truly, and loss fully, requires a similar task of simultaneity: recognizing losses when we see them, and recognizing the connections between these losses.

The following pages are my attempt to locate these cairns that, seen through the lens of grief and tragedy, point toward how we might allow fire to reinhabit the West, and how we might reinhabit a land that burns. I focus on the American West because this is where my stories reside, where my relationship with fire

1 | WINDS

The wind blows to the south,
        and goes round to the north;
round and round goes the wind,
        and on its circuits the wind returns.
        —Ecclesiastes 1:6

When the prevailing downriver wind (call it Wind Number One)
first struck the promontory near the mouth of Meriwether Canyon,
it split as if it had struck a big rock in a river and part of it (Wind
Number Two) went straight ahead over the promontory and then
straight down it in eddies on the Mann Gulch side.
        —Norman Maclean, *Young Men and Fire*

Deep within the brain of every rookie firefighter are branded the
words *fuel, weather,* and *topography*—the godhead of fire behavior. No forest or range fire burns apart from the influence of
these factors. Among the three, weather is the most variable, and
as a constituent of weather, wind reigns supreme. My story of
fire and loss, and how I've come to understand both in relation
to the West, begins with wind, or more like winds: one wind
whipping through a central Montana canyon that forty-five years
later I would trace with a blue felt pen in a classroom in Prineville, Oregon; a second wind that would sweep over the west
slope of the Colorado Rockies on a hot July day in 1994 then dif-

fuse throughout the West like a great lamentation. These winds were weathervanes, pointing toward other winds that were only barely rustling the lee side of my consciousness.

JUNE 15, 1994

The fan in the overhead projector squealed like an injured rabbit (compliments of the Crook County High School audio-visual department). On a scratched plastic sheet I drew an arrow snaking down the impounded waters of the Missouri River, down Holter Lake toward Mann Gulch and the Gates of the Mountains, or as Meriwether Lewis first called them in 1805, "the gates of the rocky mountains."[1] My arrow represented wind. I explained how at least one theory of the August 5, 1949, "blowup" of the Mann Gulch fire is based on wind. In this account, wind funneling down the Missouri River canyon carried embers into bone-dry tinder near the mouth of Mann Gulch, creating spotfires that coalesced in an ocean of flame. This wall of fire moved upcanyon, ever faster, ever hotter, eventually overtaking those firefighters caught in its path. A blowup, in this sense, is not a literal explosion like the seemingly instantaneous blast from a bundle of dynamite; it's a moment in a fire's history when fuel, weather, and topography contribute to the rapid transition of a low-intensity, slow-moving fire to a fast-moving inferno. With enough heat and atmospheric instability, a fire's plume at this stage can even overpower local winds, creating its own weather.

For as long as I'd fought fire, the federal government's canned training material on fire safety had labeled Mann Gulch a classic "tragedy fire"—that is, a fire in which fatalities occurred fitting a typical pattern. Mann Gulch was also described as an impetus for developing the Ten Standard Fire Orders in 1957, essentially the Decalogue of wildland fire safety. In today's format, the orders look something like this:

1. Keep informed on fire weather conditions and forecasts.
2. Know what your fire is doing at all times.
3. Base all actions on current and expected behavior of the fire.
4. Identify escape routes and safety zones, and make them known.
5. Post lookouts when there is possible danger.
6. Be alert. Keep calm. Think clearly. Act decisively.
7. Maintain prompt communications with your forces, your boss and adjoining forces.
8. Give clear instructions and be sure they are understood.
9. Maintain control of your forces at all times.
10. Fight fire aggressively, having provided for safety first.

This was the first time that I'd formally discussed Mann Gulch before a group. My presentation on "general and local winds" was part of the Prineville District of the Bureau of Land Management's fire behavior training. Earlier in the spring, I'd read the literary scholar Norman Maclean's book *Young Men and Fire* and was intrigued by his attempt to explain and add flesh to an otherwise anonymous—though organizationally significant —tragedy. Lest our crew become jaded by the same dated video-tapes, slides, and overhead transparencies that we subjected them to year after year, I decided to share a few excerpts from *Young Men and Fire* and diagram Maclean's theory of wind as a case in point of elementary fire weather.

So, in the stuffy classroom that only a few days earlier had witnessed soliloquies by Macbeth, I tried to wax eloquent, in Maclean's words, about fire and death. A couple of kids tossed a basketball to each other in the back of the room; a few heads, still aimed toward the screen, rested on folded arms; one or two of the group wrote something in their workbooks. I tried to make the deaths of twelve Missoula smokejumpers and one Forest Service fire guard intelligible and impress on this year's crew —some rookies, some veterans—to never forget the basics of fire behavior.

"Mann Gulch isn't that much different from the river drainages around Maupin, Paulina, or Dayville," I said.

Maybe I took myself too seriously; maybe I wasn't serious enough. Either way, the prelunch audience drifted in and out of consciousness.

Several other supervisors and I had hoped to travel to Mann Gulch to videotape the terrain. It's one thing to read about places that cradled tragedy; it's another to maintain one's balance on an angled slope of cured bunchgrass and feel one's calves burn under the weight of a backpack in the midday sun. To be where life ceased is to stand on sacred ground, a rupture in the universe.

The mother of a deceased firefighter on the South Canyon fire said it best: "I feel closer to him here than I do to him in the cemetery where he is buried. This is the last place that he was alive."[2] We were convinced that one way to disrupt complacency was to link realities of death to possibilities in our own backyard, areas that shared bunchgrass, cheatgrass, a few scattered trees, and acres of loose rock. Fires that kill do not inhabit some mythic lair—happening to someone else, a long ways away, in big timber and heavy fuel, far removed from water. They have occurred overlooking the Missouri River amidst rock scree and grass; they could also flare up along the breaks of the Deschutes or John Day Rivers or, as we would soon realize, above an interstate highway paralleling the Colorado River, in a thicket of Gambel oak and piñon-juniper. But I'm getting ahead of myself. First came Mann Gulch, Maclean's book, and my attempt to make Maclean's theory on wind relevant to the inevitable fires we would face in the weeks to come in Oregon's high desert.

JULY 6, 1994

Almost a month had elapsed since our district fire crew began its summer tour of duty. The week following our classroom sessions at Crook County High, we camped out in green canvas cabin tents at Jimmy McCuen Spring, a natural seep bubbling from a forty-acre plot of BLM land adjoining the Snow Mountain District of the Ochoco National Forest. This was "fire camp." There we practiced digging handline and slicing face-cuts in juniper trees. We extinguished practice fires, learned how to shoot azimuths, and ate artery-plugging meals of bacon, sausage, well-marbled beef, and barbecued, yellow-fatted carcasses of whole fryers, all washed down with whole milk, coffee, and smuggled Hamm's beer.

For most of the crew, field training ended abruptly with reports of and dispatches to actual fires burning 150 miles to our northwest, in the northern half of the Prineville District. One fire burned in a sage-choked feeder canyon of Buck Hollow Creek, a tributary to the Deschutes River. A second was reported to our dispatch office as threatening the small town of Antelope, a late-1800s stage stop and the mid-1980s serfdom of the India-born guru Bhagwan Shree Rajneesh. Neither fire amounted to much, other than auguring an early start to a potentially over-time-rich summer. More fires—all fairly benign—followed on their heels.

At the time, I served as crew foreman at Bakeoven Guard Station, in Maupin, Oregon. Maupin (pronounced "mop-in"), population 480, sits on a slanting basalt bench above the Deschutes River—a seasonal boomtown of self-bailing rafts, elk-hair caddis, graphite rods, and day-glow thongs. Our station, a stubby single-wide mobile home rescued by the BLM from its heritage within the Federal Emergency Management Agency (a sign below one of the eaves read "For Disaster Relief Only"), sat vacant for a week: our well had tested positive for *E. coli.* So while we waited for a jugful of Purex to do its work, the BLM was so generous as to put my three-person crew and me up in the Deschutes

Motel, a ranch-style honey with a half dozen rooms and a complimentary view of the old mill site on the west side of town.

During the heat of the day we alternated between patrolling the recently controlled fires, reoutfitting our yellow fire engines with hose, tools, and MRES (those delectable, plastic-bagged military "Meals Ready to Eat"), cruising along the washboarded Deschutes River access road to discourage the public from building open fires, and inventorying this summer's swimwear.

Every day cauliflower-shaped cumulus inched farther north. Clouds that earlier in the week sprouted near the California border today blossomed into full-blown cumulonimbus as far north as Bend and Redmond and Prineville. Within another day their anvil-shaped tops would overtake Maupin, Grass Valley, and Condon. Throughout the West, thunderheads had already welled up, dropping down stringers of brilliant light that reciprocated upward in columns of drifting smoke.

One lucky bastard—the crew foreman at our Dayville station —got an assignment to Colorado as a strike team leader—which could mean supervising five fire engines, two twenty-person hand crews, or two bulldozers. The rest of us held down the 2.5-million-acre fort of our district.

In the morning we checked the Box Elder fire, thirty miles north of Maupin along the Deschutes. "No smokes," I radioed to dispatch. "Probably won't be coming out here tomorrow." Back in Maupin, dinner consisted of yet another greasy, per diem–subsidized meal at the Deschutes River Inn. By 6 PM the temperature was almost bearable, having at last dropped below ninety, but still hotter than hell in my tiny motel room, where I sat sweating on the edge of the bed, my bare feet dangling into a warm sea of azure shag.

More out of habit than anything, I turned on the national news: a little white noise to accompany an only marginally cool Hamm's from my ice chest now half full of only marginally cool water. Even through the green-tinted Zenith, I could make out footage of fire and smoke, accompanied by a soundbite announcing firefighter fatalities in Colorado. The anchor reported several confirmed fatalities and several firefighters still missing on the South Canyon fire, a fire on the south flank of Storm King Mountain, near Glenwood Springs.

I bolted out my open door to tell the rest of the crew to turn on the news. Three other half-dressed firefighters greeted me on the concrete sidewalk, on the same mission. We all convened in my sweatbox and continued watching the coverage. Some of those killed were members of a twenty-person Forest Service Hotshot crew based out of Prineville, Oregon. I would soon learn that earlier in the day winds associated with a dry cold front had frothed a smoldering pain-in-the-ass fire into a roiling blowup that consumed fourteen lives. A month ago we had used Mann Gulch as an object lesson to bridge similarities in fuel type, topography, and weather between the Gates of the Mountains and central Oregon. That was as far as any of us hoped the analogy would ever go. Yet the lessons of mortality would grind deep as the day turned to dusk. Death had come home: half of a hometown crew could be killed just as easily as young smokejumpers a half century ago.

Initially some TV and radio newscasts reported the fatalities as being Prineville BLM firefighters. Needless to say, district crews frantically phoned family members to assure them that we were still safely in Oregon. But the Dayville Guard Station foreman was in Colorado. Eventually word trickled in that he was safe, for which we were deeply relieved. Still, firefighters like us had been killed. Others were missing but would soon be found dead. This was Wednesday—or, as I scrawled in my Smokey Bear calendar book, "Black Wed."

JULY 7, 1994

The next morning two messages rolled out of our station's fax machine. The first, on U.S. Department of the Interior letterhead, was from Steve Lent, our district fire management officer. It was the Prineville Interagency Hotshot crew's manifest, listing personnel, flight weights, and incident command positions of crew members. Numbers 2 through 10 were circled, with a note identifying these as the victims. The second message was a news release from Oregon's governor, Barbara Roberts. It ordered that all U.S. and Oregon flags at state facilities be flown at half-mast for the following nine days. The statement continued:

> The heartfelt condolences of every Oregonian should go out to the families and loved ones of the nine brave firefighters from our state who died in Colorado yesterday.

All too often, we take for granted the work done every year by thousands of firefighters from Oregon and across the western states. We seldom acknowledge the backbreaking labor and tremendous risks these dedicated men and women accept each time they step up to a fire-line to protect our forests and our homes.

They offer us a magnificent service, and sometimes, as with these nine Oregonians, they give the ultimate sacrifice—their lives. We must never forget their heroism, and we must never forget the tragedy of this loss.

I posted both faxes on a cork bulletin board above the telephone, lowered the U.S. flag at the Bakeoven Guard Station to half-mast, and began the drive back to Prineville for a briefing on the Colorado incident.

Twenty-five of us from Maupin, Dayville, Paulina, and Prineville—all our stations—crammed into the crew weight room, waiting for Steve to bring us any scrap of news on what was going on a thousand miles to our southeast. He read a tentative chronology of the preceding day's events. The fire's name was South Canyon, though it actually was burning on the flanks of Storm King Mountain, not in South Canyon as originally reported. A passing cold front brought high winds that led to a blowup that overran fourteen firefighters on a side ridge of Storm King. Robert had called and was safe, though he had been reassigned as a line scout on the fire following the blowup. Some survivors had deployed fire shelters. Few other details were available. Steve read the circled names on the manifest: Jon Kelso,

Kathi Beck, Scott Blecha, Levi Brinkley, Bonnie Holtby, Rob Johnson, Tami Bickett, Doug Dunbar, Terri Hagen. Muffled sobs came from several bowed heads.

"I don't know that I could handle even one person being killed off this crew," Steve said. "No fire is worth getting hurt over, or worse. For God's sake, if you don't feel comfortable with a fire, pull back!"

At some level, we all heard Steve's safety admonitions and couldn't agree more. I appreciated the almost parental concern for our well-being. But most of our minds were elsewhere. We were thinking about the firefighters in Colorado, many of whom we knew and on occasion worked with, some of whom would return to Oregon in sealed caskets.

There would be a parade on Saturday, an annual part of Prineville's big rodeo to-do for the year, the Crooked River Roundup. Normally the fire crew would take part in the off-duty festivities by laying down bets at the horse races, soaking up pitchers of cheap beer at the Waterhole or Cinnabar, or enjoying time with family and friends before the cheatgrass fully cured and thunderstorms became a daily occurrence that would take us away for weeks at a time to the margins of wildfires.

Steve said that we could walk in Saturday's parade—the organizer had invited all local and regional firefighters to take part. After the parade, there would be a memorial service. He told us to wear firepants and fireshirts (those yellow or green outfits made from fire-resistant fabric called Nomex) or crew t-shirts if we joined the procession; regardless, everyone was on duty, since thunderstorms with high lightning-activity levels were fore-casted. We left the weight room but very quickly gravitated into small groups to exchange rumors and theories about South Canyon. To share our anxiety.

JULY 9, 1994

Throughout the early morning hours lightning peppered a trail across central and eastern Oregon. Sometime after midnight my phone rang. It was our dispatcher. "Want to go to a fire?" he asked. I didn't, but said yes anyway, which is what seasonal firefighters are always taught to do. The fire was reported to be burning in a side drainage of the Deschutes River Canyon. The Grass Valley Rural Fire Department was on the scene but re-quested BLM assistance. So in the darkness of Saturday morning four yellow fire engines (really just one-ton trucks with utility boxes and 200-gallon water tanks) caravanned up U.S. Highway 97 en route to a five-acre blaze of grass and sage burning near the head of Smith Canyon. By the time we arrived, the rural boys had more or less contained the fire, showering what water they had over the smoldering hillside.

I'd hoped we could mop up the fire early in the morning and still have enough time to make the two-hour return trip to Prine-ville for the memorial service at Crook County High School's outdoor stadium. Deep down I knew this was wishful thinking, as the mop-up yielded a bumper crop of sparking sagebrush stumps along the fire's perimeter. The Grass Valley firefighters went home to catch some breakfast and shut-eye. A little later the two Prineville engines returned to their station, leaving my crew to finish mopping up and babysitting what seemed more of an annoyance than a threat.

I later learned that the parade included nine riderless horses, from whose empty saddles fluttered blue ribbons. After the horses came a flatbed covered with tree boughs, nine American flags, a wreath of yellow flowers, and a white heart. Finally came the mourners: survivors from the Prineville Hotshots, families, and any firefighters—federal, state, rural, or city—who wanted to show their support and solidarity by walking in the parade. The procession continued down Third Street through the center of town, then to the stadium.

Some people commented on how they thought the riderless horses were sort of corny. Maybe they were, but true grieving is never orchestrated. While riderless horses probably have more in common with nineteenth-century cavalry regiments than contemporary firefighters, in a town where the high school teams are the Cowboys and many residents—whether they've ridden horses or not—overwhelmingly prefer Wranglers and cowboy boots, a horse without rider is probably one of the truest symbols of loss. And to the extent that firefighting often remains linked to war and battle, a symbol of fallen warriors (the riderless horse) is understandable.

While my crew grubbed around in ashes and charcoal on the west side of Smith Canyon, others sat in the blue-and-yellow outdoor bleachers and listened to eulogies: from Todd Valley, mayor of Prineville; Roy Romer, governor of Colorado; Barbara Roberts, governor of Oregon; Bob Zanella, mayor of Glenwood Springs; Tom Schmidt, Ochoco National Forest supervisor; and Art Currier, Prineville District ranger.

For many, the service was cut short by a new fire. In an eerie recapitulation of the tragic pall that had obscured the west slope of the Rockies three days earlier, smoke curled up from behind a rimrock-capped mesa southeast of town: a fire in the Maury Mountains. Firefighters in the audience—prompted by pagers, taps on the shoulder from supervisors, and intuition—rose in preparation for blazes that by day's end would commit all fire suppression resources in the region. The memorial service, framed by billowing smoke, was a reminder that, at least on this day, sackcloth and ashes would have to be worn on the margin of a going fire.

I regret not making it to that service, but by midafternoon I'd almost forgotten that Prineville existed. Our fire, a seemingly dead-out smudge, erupted into what three days later would amount to a ten-thousand-acre swath of blackened sage, bunchgrass, and cured winter wheat.

| PART II

Lightning, the crackling demon of the skies that causes chills of apprehension to course up and down the spines of foresters in the hot, dry months, is going to be attacked in Region 1 of the Forest Service this summer.

Research is the tool to be used and the goal is to learn if it is possible to prevent or reduce lightning fires by weather modification.

—Gerald G. Alquist, *Missoula Sentinel*, 1953

Fires had to be controlled. You couldn't just start a fire anywhere. Fire can do a lot of harm or a lot of good. You have to know how to control it. . . . It has been a long time since my father and my uncles used to burn each spring. But we were told to stop. The Mounties arrested some people. . . . The country has changed from what it used to be—brush and trees where there used to be lots of meadows and not so many animals as before.

—Seventy-six-year-old Cree Indian

We can't be sure why they came. We aren't even sure exactly when they came. But sometime during the last great ice age, probably between 12,000 and 35,000 years ago, people entered Beringia, the land bridge and adjoining ice-free areas connecting eastern Asia with Alaska and northwest Canada.[1] Maybe they were on hunting forays in search of greener Pleistocene pastures. Maybe they simply felt cramped by too many neighbors or unsavory in-laws. Whatever their reasons, they began one of the final chapters in human expansion around the earth. And with them they brought the final expansion of fire.

For thousands of years, ice-free Beringia was isolated from the rest of North America by two massive glaciers. The Cordilleran Ice Sheet extended south from the Alaska Range to the Alexander Archipelago of southeast Alaska, then along the Pacific Ocean all the way to the Olympic Mountains of Washington State. Fingerlike lobes drooped into Washington, Idaho, and Montana. From its southeast border along the Continental Divide, the Cordilleran Sheet hooked north on a line roughly paralleling the Canadian Rockies and the Alberta–British Columbia border. Finally, it cut through northwest British Columbia, southern Yukon, and back into Alaska. The Laurentide Ice Sheet pressed against the eastern edge of the Cordilleran Sheet, extending across Canada all the way to the Atlantic and as far south as the northern-tier states and New England.

Scattered alpine glaciers dotted many ranges south of these sheets. Like ribbons of inlaid silver, they flowed down the slopes of the Pacific Coast Range, the Cascades and Rockies, the Elkhorns, Wallowas, Steens, and Bitterroots. Then, around 18,000 years ago, the glaciers began to recede.[2]

By 15,000 years ago, the sutures binding the Cordilleran and Laurentide Ice Sheets had ripped open, creating an ice-free passageway from eastern Beringia to the center of the continent. Archaeological evidence suggests that people were living in interior North America by at least 11,500 years ago, most likely entering through this solid Northwest Passage from Alaska to Montana.[3]

When the first Americans (the initial Corps of Discovery) pressed south, they passed between great walls of ice, and with their passing they brought the skill and technology of fire—a "torch" that would spread beyond their fire pits to shape entire landscapes for the next ten millennia before dimming to a weak flicker.

The first Americans encountered a land that was both similar to and different from what we see in the West today. With the exception of occasional landscape-altering volcanic eruptions (such as Mount Mazama 6,000 years ago) and some climatic variation, "environmental conditions in the intermontane Northwest remained relatively stable for at least [the last] 10,000 years."[4] All of today's familiar native plant species were present, although not, of course, those exotic species later introduced by Europeans. Dominant tree species date back as far as 30 million to 60 million years.[5]

Yet even though today's plant species carpeted the late Pleistocene landscape, their distribution, local abundance, and composition were different. Here it's worth taking a slight, though important, digression into ecological theory. Not that long ago, the plant ecologist Frederic Clements's theory of ecological succession was widely accepted. According to Clements, species moved in discrete communities over time and space. For instance, if a piece of ground was scoured by a receding glacier or leveled by a fire, certain pioneering species like lupine or fireweed would initially take root in the disturbed site. They would prepare the seedbed for other species by fixing nitrogen or creating microclimates. Groups of species better able to compete for these resources, or maybe for sunlight, would succeed the first. This process would progress in a more-or-less lockstep manner, certain species always being associated with one another in mutually beneficial relationships and succeeded by other groups that possessed a competitive advantage, until a "climax" state was reached. Theoretically, the climax community would be "self-replicating and would continue indefinitely unless disturbed by some catastrophe, such as clearing or firing."[6]

Today, although the idea of succession still has its place in ecology, the notion that plants exist as discrete, mutually dependent communities controlled solely by climate has taken a beating.[7] It is now acknowledged that species respond much more individualistically to their environments than was once thought.[8] Hence, the land that the first Americans entered, while hosting familiar species, may have been arranged differently than today. This point will prove crucial a little later as we think about the love triangle of fire, the land, and the peoples that first encountered that land.

While flora was comparable, fauna differed markedly. Not that animals that exist now didn't exist then, but the land the first Americans entered was also home to giant ground sloths, giant bison, camels, and horses. That these species went extinct is without doubt; why they went extinct is less clear. Some scientists hypothesize that the climate of the waning Ice Age precipitated their demise; others allege overhunting by the newly arrived humans; still others suggest a combination of climate change, overhunting, and landscape modifications brought on by human-caused fire. Regardless, these species, along with at least seventy genera of animal life in America, soon went extinct.[9]

These first peoples entered a land in western Montana, northern Idaho, and eastern Washington recently scoured by enormous floods triggered by receding glaciers that previously had dammed lakes such as Lake Columbia and Lake Missoula. Many of these first peoples would have entered northern Montana just east of the Continental Divide, between the Cordilleran and Laurentide Sheets, near the lapping waters of Glacial Lake Great Falls.[10] Today we probably see Holter Lake (the inundated portion of the Missouri River between the Gates of the Mountains) as a testament to twentieth-century engineering. In reality, Holter is a minor recapitulation of an Ice Age impoundment that stretched all the way from Helena to just northwest of Great Falls.

Along that stretch of water lies Mann Gulch, a small canyon whose rocky north side now cradles bunchgrass, a few blackened snags, a few ridgeline ponderosa, white concrete crosses, and painful memories of a hot day in August 1949. In the region north of Mann Gulch, those with the power to kindle fire emerged from the ice. In Mann Gulch, firefighters tried to evict fire, at a very high price. Like all attempts to draw ironies out of time and space, my lacing together fire's entry and exit may be nothing more than tracing the shapes of animals in cumulus suspended in a blue summer sky. But I think it's more than projection or hyperbole to say that over eleven thousand years ago, fire—be it actual hot embers or fire-making implements—passed through a gap in the ice, then, in time, along the shores of a sprawling lake very similar to one today, near a dry gulch whose slopes would claim the lives of thirteen young men trying to extinguish the residue of lightning.

One of the winds that swayed my understanding of loss and fire, and the tragedy of forgetting tragedy, blew through the area where human-made fire first entered the midcontinent and through which it would also depart, both symbolically and to some degree literally, as a result of aggressive fire suppression. To understand loss, we must first come to know origins of the thing to be lost: those people who brought fire with them to the American West, and the fires that preceded them, which were legion. This is no idle antiquarianism. Human-initiated fire is a relative newcomer in the history of North America. And though the modern story of fire is a story of loss marked by four cairns, fire will never be fully extirpated from the landscapes of the West.

Every elementary school child knows that if you place a Mason jar over a lit candle, the flame soon goes out, for fire needs three things to burn. First, it needs the fuel supplied by the wax and wick. Second, it requires the heat generated by the match. Finally, fire needs oxygen, that ethereal element whose presence is validated when the jar descends over the wick and the flickering flame contracts into a smoking, impotent black string. So, too, as long as North America nurtured life that baked under a hot summer sun, and as long as lightning penetrated the primeval atmosphere to mingle with shrubs and trees and cured yellow grass, there was fire. Native fire. First fire. Indigenous fire.

Such fire would have roamed freely wherever and whenever fuel and weather allowed. Spring lightning strikes might have split junipers apart or spiraled down the jigsaw-puzzled bark of yellow-bellied ponderosa, but these damp and cool months wouldn't have birthed much fire. If a tree's core was rotted out or filled with dry rat scat, or if its base sheltered crispy tinder, lightning might produce a small smolder that would seethe within the tree's gut until chilly nights, high humidities, and soaking rains extinguished it. Stillborn. A little later in the spring or early summer, a fire might actually creep away from its point of conception, or continue baking until a parched summer breeze propelled it across the landscape. Freed from the tinkering of shovels, bulldozers, and retardant bombers, the only thing holding back these fires would have been natural barriers (like rivers, rockslides, or meadows) or changes in weather that would once again send embers into partial hibernation. Eventually, such free-burning, free-spirited fires would either go out on their own or hunker in roots and gnarled trunks until weather conditions changed, sending them sprawling over the landscape again. Throughout the year, any given fire might alternate through several cycles of simmering to blazing to simmering.[11]

Indigenous fire wouldn't have been any more homogeneous across the landscape than it is today. If anything, it would have been even more spotty and mosaic because more frequent and extensive fires engendered more variation: areas of heavy fuel concentrations that might serve as hiding spots for hibernating fire; areas of sparse fuel, created by fire, that when ablaze would be highly susceptible to variable weather conditions—to fire's benefit and demise. High elevations have only narrow windows of time, between spring thaw and fall snows, during which fire can truly erupt. In years of heavy snowpack and late thaw, virtually no chance exists for fires to extend beyond a lightning-struck subalpine fir into lush alpine meadows.

Over millions of years, plant species evolved in this seasonal hearth that spanned a continent, a hearth rekindled by lightning and vivified by weather. If there would be fires was not the question. How vegetation would survive in an environment that burned was. Some species evolved the ability for individual plants to resist fire. Take ponderosa pine, for instance. Its thick bark, even at a fairly young age, allows it to withstand low- to medium-intensity fires. With age, ponderosas shed their lower branches ("self-pruning," some call it), which eliminates a possible "ladder" for fire to spread from the ground to the tree's crown. Also, many shrubs and perennial grasses sprout "basally" from their root crowns or from below-ground stems. This allows them to endure the hot amputation of their above-ground parts while surviving to see another season.

Still other species, like lodgepole pine, actually depend on fire to regenerate. Since stands of lodgepole often grow close and thick, crown fires are more easily generated and sustained than in a widely spaced stand of ponderosa. But that's okay because lodgepole's relation to fire is not one of resistance by individual trees, but resistance by the species. The mechanism lies in what's called "serotiny." Certain subspecies of lodgepole possess serotinous—that is, closed—cones, and only with high temperatures associated with fire or intense sunlight do these cones open and release seed. After the 1988 fires in Yellowstone National Park left many people steaming with disgust over a national treasure reduced to smoking black snags, no sooner had the ashes cooled than lodgepole seeds descended to the ground and then began stirring in their mineral soil bed. Today small trees blanket the ground in an ocean of needled green.[12]

In arid regions of the West, if it weren't for occasional fire, nutrients would freeze in the aging hulks of trees and brush and rank mats of grass, or in the lifeless skeletons of prostrate trees. It's different along the coast. I've never felt comfortable in the lush temperate rainforests of the Pacific Northwest; I've always felt as if I were decomposing with the land around me. Nevertheless, there is a certain ecological elegance in water's ability to nurture decay, recycling the dead. What dies rots, and what rots sinks into the ground, where, with the alchemy of sunlight and water, nutrients harden into plants that will again reach toward heaven. But in the Intermountain West, where precipitation is sporadic and skimpy, decomposition is slow. Fire speeds up the process.

Animals don't self-prune or possess serotinous gonads, but many animals do thrive on fire's effects. Deer and elk congregate in fresh burns to lick salts released by the heat or to nibble on

[27]

new shoots of grass. Track the regrowth of a burn into the following season and you may find these same ungulates browsing on the tender regrowth of fire-pruned shrubs. Some birds, like woodpeckers, utilize the rotted cavities of burnt snags as homes. The list could go on.

Because of this symbiosis between fire and many organisms, it's questionable whether fire should even be called a "disturbance," as it's often characterized. True enough, fire brings about change, and if *disturbance* is synonymous with *change*, then the term is appropriate. However, if disturbance implies the upsetting of order—a knocking out of balance a harmonious system—then the term seems less than adequate. To the extent that organisms depend on fire, fire is no more of a disturbance than water or sunlight, though not nearly as ubiquitous or necessary for day-to-day survival.

In sum, whether cheating death individually or as a species, vegetation in America—indeed, throughout the world—has evolved ways to cope with, even thrive on, fire.[13] For a time, heat-sensitive species will disappear when submerged under the flames of summer. But even before the ashes cool, a succession of life begins to unfurl. To the extent that individual organisms, species, and interrelationships between individuals and species have become inscribed by patterns of fire, change the regimen of fire and the communities of plants and animals will also change. For thousands of years people added their own fires to the seasonal blazes of the West. Then came a people for whom fire was an annoyance, an impediment, a disturbance that brought about all manner of loss to the things they valued. From the standpoint of fire, the last 150 years of American history have been like an oxygen-starved hearth, a slow smother. I discovered wisps of this loss in the basement of the Missoula Federal Building.

HISTORICAL: INDIANS—NORTHERN REGION

That was the title of the file folder I was rifling through in the U.S. Forest Service's Northern Region archives, in Missoula, Montana. I was looking for old photos or newspaper clippings related to American Indian use of fire. I didn't find much, just two black-and-white photographs taken by someone named W. E. Steuerwald and dated September 1956. Still, they were arresting—two long-buried promotional shots that captured the irony of western fire history, of fire flowing south between ice into a land indigenous with fire that ten millennia later would sprout crosses on a hill, crosses dedicated to those trying to extinguish fire.

One photograph shows an elderly Chief Charlo of the Confederated Salish and Kootenai Tribes wearing full ceremonial dress: feather-rimmed headdress and shield, beaded shirt and leggings. On his left stands a homespun Smokey Bear—bunched-up hair shirt tucked into his denim pants, held up tight by a cinched "Smokey" belt buckle. He stands erect, feet slightly parted, holding a new shovel in his left paw. On his head (which stretches a good foot above the others in the picture) sits a droopy fedora emblazoned with "Smokey." Next to the bear stands a smiling little boy, identified as "son of Indian Service employee." He holds a small sign, half his height, showing a picture of Smokey and his friends and the words "PLEASE BE CAREFUL . . . PREVENT FOREST FIRES." Mrs. Charlo stands behind the boy. She wears a scarf tied firm over her hair and a dark-colored shawl, embossed with roses, draped over her shoulders. She stares emotionless at the lens of Steuerwald's camera. Finally, an unnamed man in a suit and tie, identified only as "Superintendent of Flathead Indian Reservation," stands to the right of Mrs. Charlo, smiling approvingly on the Flathead's poster child of fire safety.

The other photo shows Chief Charlo, his wife, and Smokey. The chief shakes hands with Smokey while looking over his shoulder away from the bear. Smokey looks toward the obviously distracted chief. Mrs. Charlo looks past Smokey toward whatever her husband watches. Maybe nothing. Maybe a distant smoke signal nearly extinguished.

It's all so ironic . . . and staged. A bipedal bear—creation of the U.S. Forest Service and icon of the National Ad Council—enlists the help of the Salish-Kootenai tribal leader in a war against fire, an element of the cosmos that Charlo's people had handled and lived amidst for eons.

For nearly sixty years Smokey has stared down his ursine paw and fed us a lie: "Only you can prevent forest fires." This couldn't be further from the truth. I said earlier that as long as lightning and cured tinder have commingled across the face of North America there has been fire; similarly, as long as humans have resided upon that seasonally smoking plain there have been additional fires, many intentionally set, some not. For most of the past century, however, the history of fire in the West was at best poorly understood, at worst negligently denied. For many the issue boiled down to a seemingly self-evident syllogism:

The most valuable thing about forests is trees.
Fire destroys trees.
Therefore, to preserve forests, fire must be eliminated.

Never mind that indigenous fire had seasonally rekindled for millions of years, and that to thoroughly eliminate human-caused fires would require the elimination of those indigenous peoples whose subsistence, as I'll describe shortly, depended on fire. It's difficult to disentangle mere ecological ignorance from the philosophical commitment that sees death as an unqualified evil, even the death of trees; it's also difficult to separate historical ignorance of native people's use of fire from sheer cultural chauvinism—as if American Indians were too simpleminded or stupid to ever intentionally use fire. As Stephen Pyne has written, "The evidence for aboriginal burning in nearly every landscape of North America is so conclusive, and the consequences of fire suppression so visible, that it seems fantastic that a debate about whether Indians used broadcast fire or not should ever have taken place."[14] Fantastic, maybe; true nonetheless.

Blame for the skimpiness of our knowledge of indigenous people's fire practices should at least partially be shouldered by anthropologists who for most of the twentieth century ignored the impact that hunter-gatherers had on their surroundings.[15]

The prevailing logic assumed that meager populations of natives, armed with their primitive technologies, could never have altered the landscape in fundamental ways. Stephen Pyne again: "Enchanted by the powerful mirage of the virgin forest myth, historians also ignored aboriginal fire."[16] The first European explorers and settlers entered a land that appeared unchanged from the first chapter of Genesis. But it wasn't. According to the writer Alston Chase, "the land that the early settlers found in the West . . . was not made that way by God alone, but partly by man. The Indians, too, knew how to play God, and one of the tools with which they made their Eden was fire."[17]

By the time Captains Lewis and Clark poled their way up the Missouri, fast-spreading diseases such as smallpox and measles, carried across the continent by the first European explorers and trappers, had already depopulated much of the American West. Some estimate the precontact native population of North America as high as 10 million, and the population throughout the Americas upwards of 100 million.[18] Most likely, when populations peaked, so did fire. Partial evidence for this was bequeathed by the wane of the Ice Age.

As soon as glaciers receded from the spine of Montana's Bitterroot Mountains some 12,000 years ago, a small pond and eventually a bog developed at what is now Lost Trail Pass near the Idaho-Montana border. Sediment samples taken from the bog show evidence of fire shortly after the glaciers disappeared. And sediments representing the last 2,000 years show a drastic increase in charcoal—more than for the previous 9,500 years combined.[19] But why? Did the weather turn markedly warmer and drier, or was lightning more frequent, sparking more fires? Probably neither. Did plant communities develop that were more prone to fire? Maybe.

One likely reason for this increase in ash is an increase in human-caused fires. Though people fanned out across the Intermountain West at least 10,000 years ago, could it be that the torch that flowed south—between the ice, past Glacial Lake Great Falls and the Gates of the Mountains—had, by 2,000 years ago, spread to enough hands in the southern Bitterroot Valley that a previous trickle of fire became a flood? If so, then to the indigenous fires of southwest Montana came the fires of indigenous peoples, swelling over time, then crashing on the rocks of disease and the U.S. Cavalry.[20]

As a tool, fire has effects disproportionate to the number of hands wielding it: one spark from a torch under the right conditions can send fire skipping beyond the horizon for days to follow. This fact may lead to what the geographer Thomas Vale has called the "myth of the humanized landscape," as if admitting that humans have influenced their environments in all regions of North America is the same thing as saying that all landscapes were "monolithically humanized"—an environmental non sequitur. Vale argues that acknowledging the fact that the Miwok peoples burned in California's Yosemite Valley "is not sufficient to support the claim that such burning altered the fundamental character of the landscape."[21]

As it was in California, so it was throughout the West. During the summer months a watershed becomes a "fireshed": humans, water, and fire all prefer to travel through channels, and the higher in elevation you go, the less concentrated all three become. The fires of indigenous peoples also flowed through channels. But to admit that native peoples used fire throughout America is not to say that fires were spread evenly over the land. Not far from Lost Trail Pass Bog in the southern Bitterroot Valley, evidence suggests otherwise. Through comparing fire scars on the oldest trees in his study area, the fire historian and forester Stephen Barrett discovered that prior to the 1860s, fires were not only more frequent overall than they are today but were also more frequent in valley bottoms. He attributed this phenomenon to settlement patterns. Native Americans in the Bitterroots located their major encampments on the valley floors, so presumably most of their fires would have been set near those encampments. But like the flue of a stove, canyons funnel smoke and heat and fire toward their headwaters. Given enough force and momentum, fire may overflow its banks, and the banks of fire are the limits of fuel. While streams forge their way to the ocean, fire claws its way to high mountain cirques, running perpendicular to drainages, over ridgetops, or flowing in wind-driven waves beyond narrow channels.

Hence, flooding over the fires that resulted from lightning's hot blast were streams of human-caused fires (both intentionally set and accidental), concentrating where people lived, though sometimes spreading to the backcountry.[22] In 1891, under pressure from the U.S. government, the last of the Bitterroot Salish relocated from their ancestral home in the Bitterroot Valley to the Flathead Indian Reservation, over sixty miles to the north. As the Salish traveled north between the Sapphire and Bitterroot mountains, over the Higgins Street Bridge in Missoula, then into the shadow of the Mission Mountains, their fires receded with them—a fate captured on film six decades later in an awkward handshake between an Indian chief and a man in a bear suit.

• • •

Ash in a bog and fire scars on trees confirm fire; fire frequency and location suggest human hands. Nevertheless, it's still a jump from coals in a fire pit (or an escaped campfire) to fire intentionally released on the land for subsistence. Fortunately, eyewitness accounts sharpen the focus.

Journals by explorers and chroniclers such as Lewis and Clark, George Catlin, Alfred Jacob Miller, Paul Kane, and John Wesley Powell all document human hands behind many of the smoke plumes drifting through nineteenth-century western skies.[23] Admittedly, some of these firsthand accounts of why Indians burned are questionable, as often as not based on pejorative views of the Indians and their motives. Still, the link between America's indigenous peoples and free-ranging fire is clear. In the 1870s John Wesley Powell wrote:

> Everywhere throughout the Rocky Mountain Region the explorer away from the beaten paths of civilization meets with great areas of dead forests; pines with naked arms and charred trunks attesting

to the former presence of this great destroyer. The younger forests are everywhere beset with fallen timber, attesting to the rigor of the flames, and in seasons of great drought the mountaineer sees the heavens filled with clouds of smoke.

In the main these fires are set by Indians.[24]

Just as Indian fire use varied over the land, so too did nonnative attitudes toward fire. Some settlers quickly learned the usefulness of fire to control insects, improve forage, clear land, or create defensible space against wildfire.[25] Others were more skeptical. Unfortunately, it's this skeptical lens that has, for the most part, shaped our view of Indian fire use and guided our fire policy over the last one hundred years.

Like dust devils swirling through the barely cooled ashes of the 1910 fires of the northern Rockies, controversy swirled throughout the West in 1910 over whether "light burning"—low-intensity, intentionally set fires—might actually benefit forest and range. Some dubbed this notion "Paiute forestry" or the "Indian way," recognizing that Indians had used fire for various purposes (though modern silviculture was not one of them). Timber-industry proponents of "light burning" valued low-intensity, intentionally set fires as a means of removing fuels that otherwise would build up and, when ablaze, destroy their "investments." Yet the thought of killing young trees to save others was seen by many professional foresters as rooted in greed, forsaking the future of the forest. As Stephen Pyne explains their attitude, "Light burning sought an immediate reward, the preservation of mature forests, at the expense of long-range forest values, reproduction and soil protection."[26] To these foresters, all burning—whether to reduce fuel loadings, kill annoying insects, or promote forage for livestock—smacked of frontier folk practices.

In a 1911 essay titled "Did the Indian Protect the Forest?" Warren E. Coman criticized those who would suggest that Indians used intentionally set fire to mitigate the negative effects of wildfires on forests:

> To persons conversant with the Indian nature this idea is preposterous. The Indians were nomads, who dwelt in skin teepees, and banded together in tribes, whose interest [*sic*] were always individual and tribal and never collective, as a nation or association of tribes.
>
> The systematic burning of the forests by the Indians would suggest a desire by the redmen for the preservation of the trees for future use. But the history of the Indians shows that they lived always in the present.[27]

What Coman failed to recognize was the myriad ways in which American Indians used fire beyond merely improving horse pasturage. Coman's cultural myopia was not at all isolated. In 1910 G. M. Homans, California's state forester, railed against "the theory that the debris of the forest should be burned at frequent intervals, referring to the example set by the 'untutored Indians,' as a measure of protection." A decade later, from across the Atlantic, a German commentator wrote: "It was formerly common for both Indians and white hunters to thoughtlessly set underbrush ablaze merely to scare up game, and many of such fires were propagated indefinitely. Such vandalism is at the present time limited in most places."[28] (Read: limited to minuscule reservations and pockets of unenlightened whites who failed to embrace the virtue of properly valuing trees.)

The legitimate use of fire contracted to one possible use—saving forests—and the thought that fire could accomplish that goal was quickly dismissed by most professional foresters. If fire couldn't be shown to protect and enhance trees, it should be eliminated. As a turn of the prevailing logic, to the extent that property rights were associated with certain types of work—real work, white work—and Native Americans did not "work" in this narrowly defined way, they lacked legitimacy. According to the historian Nancy Langston, "When whites complained that Indians had no right to the land because they did not work it, they did not consider burning to be work, just as they did not consider hunting, fishing, or gathering as serious labor that gave one a right to the land." Indians were either "noble savages" who were too morally pure to knowingly harm the land through burning (i.e., they wouldn't have burned), they were too "untutored" to carefully wield fire (i.e., they wouldn't know how to burn), or they used fire, but to no good end (i.e., wielding fire was not work).[29]

· · ·

I've been talking as if our only means of understanding Indian fire practices is through nineteenth-century historians and chroniclers, as if Indians, their voices, and their fires are extinct. They are not. Native peoples still use fire, even if hemmed in by treaties, private property lines, and fading oral histories.[30] And besides the journals and drawings of white explorers and set-tlers, and even with the dearth of early anthropological work on indigenous people's fire practices, we do possess firsthand ac-counts of traditional fire uses. A Karok woman from northern California relayed the following:

> Our kind of people never used the plow, they never used to grub up the ground, they never used to sow anything, except tobacco. All they used to do was to burn the brush at various places, so that some good things will grow up. That way the huckleberry bushes grow up good. . . . And sometimes they also burn where the tan oak trees are lest it be brushy where they pick up the acorns. They do not want it to burn too hard, they fear that the oak trees might burn. And sometimes they used to set fire there long ago where they saw lots of acorns on the ground, in a tanbark oak grove they made roasted unshelled acorns. They do not set fire for nothing, it is for something that they set fire for.[31]

Beyond the short list of explanations given by explorers, settlers, and early foresters for why Indians burned (such as pas-ture improvement, smoke signals, or simply escaped campfires), American Indians used fire for a whole host of reasons. At times these fire applications overlapped with the natural patterns propagated by lightning; more often than not, though, they dif-fered from natural fire regimes in seasonality, frequency, inten-sity, and location.[32] In other words, Indians employed fire "at various places, so that some good things will grow up."

These myriad uses included hunting (driving game), stimulat-ing forage for desired wildlife species, improving horse pasturage (once horses were reintroduced into the Americas by the Spanish), collecting insects, controlling pests, warring on enemies, signaling, creating travel corridors, felling trees for firewood, promoting desirable vegetation (such as berries for food or plants for medicinal use and basketry), fireproofing villages, etc. These uses would have varied by region and tribe, depending on which plant species were being modified—for example, oak trees in California or huckleberries in the Rockies.[33]

The anthropologist Henry Lewis, after interviewing northern Alberta natives, concluded that "asking a hunter his reason for burning is analogous to asking a farmer why he plows." Fire and subsistence were two sides of the same coin: to burn was to live and to live was to burn. Moreover, this indigenous knowledge was "not based on some kind of mindless, habitual practices." Rather, Lewis argued, indigenous fire knowledge was based on the observation of cause and effect in nature.[34] This place-based pragmatism arose from melding disparate fires and new lands: the torch that passed between the ice merged with the indigenous fires of North America. Scientists sometimes imply that the only way to sound knowledge is through a strict adherence to the so-called "hypothetico-deductive" method. But while correlation does not equal causation, surely the careful observations underlying American Indians' fire economy ought to count as genuine knowing—even wisdom.

Here I move slowly, for the danger of idealizing native culture is all too real. That Indians used fire—used it intentionally and skillfully to survive in North America for thousands of years—is true enough. That they always and everywhere lived on the land, and used fire upon the land, in a sustainable way is less clear.[35] Whether, and to what extent, native patterns of burning *ought* to be replicated over the landscape of the West today is even more murky.

If plant species have experienced significant evolutionary change as a result of human-caused factors—such as cultural fire practices—then part of restoring ecological integrity to land-scapes will entail restoring those cultural practices, even if they no longer serve their cultural function. Some have claimed that American Indian fire use significantly contributed to evolution-ary change in vegetation. Others have questioned the impor-tance of anthropogenic fire in altering species genetics. Based on the antiquity of dominant tree species, the ecologist Paul Ala-back asks whether ten thousand years would have been sufficient to distinguish Indian fire from natural wildfire. The answers to these questions also depend on what species we're talking about and to what extent cultural fire practices deviated from natural fire patterns and cycles.[36]

But whatever the answer to these questions, we're still left with the dissipating smoke of distant fires—real loss, painful loss, irreparable loss. Into a land of indigenous fire came people who used fire; with the loss of these people came the loss of their fires; with the loss of their fires, so too went the texture of the lands they sculpted with fire, the lands that offered up camas and huckleberry, wild rice and hazel.[37] And with the fires of their hearths, agriculture, and culture safely contained on reservations came the final push to evict fire from the West in favor of a new agriculture and culture. Alston Chase poignantly speaks of the losses associated with American Indians and Yellowstone National Park: "Created for the benefit and enjoyment of the people, it destroyed a people. Dedicated to preservation, it evicted those who had preserved it. Touted as pristine, the policy required that we forget those whose absence diminished it."[38]

Toward the end of the twentieth century, ecologists would tout the virtues of the ancient role of fire in nature. Yet in the intervening decades (and to some extent even today), a war was fought in which fire was the enemy, a personification of evil. Fire was viewed as synonymous with loss (which is partly true and will constitute the next three cairns I discuss). Whatever fire touched collapsed into black death. End of story. Timber, beauty, homes, and lives were all susceptible to the fires of summer. As I already mentioned, some people recognized the usefulness of fire—even if they failed to fully understand its ecological effects.[39] But to many early foresters and policy makers fire was an anomalous force, a disturbance whose elimination would allow nature to flourish. If we could get enough manpower, horsepower, or just plain power to the edge of a fire quickly enough, we could minimize loss. "Just put the goddamned thing out" was the battle cry. Final victory against the malignant spread of fire would not be measured by speed alone. True victory would come when that crackling demon, lightning, Prometheus' gift to earth, was driven into extinction once and for all, and cumulonimbus—lightning's womb—would never again shade the earth.

Lightning still crackles through western skies; fires still start and burn, oftentimes until fall rains and November snows drive them to extinction; and the scars of fire's eviction spiderweb the region. Scars on people. Scars on land. Scars on our souls.

Decades have passed through the hour-glass of time, and nature has long since reclothed the naked landscape with grass, shrubs and trees, but the great sacrifice of human life can never be re-placed or forgotten.

—Joe Halm, reminiscing about the fires of 1910

As for tragedy, the universe likes encores to its catastrophes and does not have to be coaxed long to repeat them.

—Norman Maclean, *Young Men and Fire*

On the anniversary of this terrible tragedy, we pause to remember the lives and the courage of the firefighters who died on Storm King Mountain as they worked to protect the things we so deeply cher-ish—our landscape, our forest, our homes and our very lives.

—Montana governor Marc Racicot

JULY 9, 1994

We thought we had the son of a bitch licked. Lisa, Trevor, Glen, and I had spent the morning and early afternoon mopping up the perimeter of what we were now calling the "Smith Canyon fire." With a measly two hundred gallons of water on the back of our four-wheel-drive engines and with a forty-five-minute turn-around time for refills from the nearest farmhouse spigot, we used what water we had sparingly. Mist the hot sagebrush stumps, dig. Mist again, chink some more. Don't bury anything:

it will just smolder in its fiery grave until it ignites roots or duff, resurrecting to the surface in running fire while you're not watching. Eventually, all that you want left is a steaming black stob. Then move on. There were still spots of white-hot ash and smoldering cow pies in the fire's interior, but the edge looked and felt secure.

By now the Grass Valley volunteers were back at their station tapping kegs in preparation for their fireman's ball later in the evening, and the Prineville engines were back at the district wareyard, their crews sharpening shovels and pulaskis (combination grubhoes/axes) and filling coolers with ice and Gatorade. The memorial service was over, and I was resigned to spending the rest of the day babysitting a black slope under a blinding sun that even reptiles hide from. Typically, on a scrubby range fire, you contain it (by smothering it, drowning it, or starving it of fuel), secure the edge, then watch. Forest fires require hour upon hour of labor-intensive mop-up, turning over deep layers of duff and litter and roots, cooling and stirring, then repeating the process until you can touch the soil with the back of your hand without getting burned. Cold-trailing. But with the exception of pockets of heavy sage, range fires along the breaks of the Deschutes or John Day Rivers require little mop-up but a lot of patience—watching and patrolling a ragged black edge, sometimes miles in length, for a day or two or three, looking for smokes that then require more grubbing and more stirring. Since our fire was small, by early afternoon we were mainly just watching.

Our rigs sat at the top of the fire amidst cold, black tufts of bunchgrass, their delicate, fire-cropped stems frozen in position like so many smudged lantern mantles. I read the newspaper while sitting in my lawn chair and occasionally peered down the hill into the heavy sage for wisps of smoke. At the other engine my crew feasted on stale MRES. Between bites of gelatinized ham tidbits they watched the west flank. Lisa and Trevor reclined on the utility boxes, and Glen, like one of Smith Canyon's reptiles, took refuge in the cab.

For a firefighter, no sound is more sickening than the sound of popping corn under a withering sun. It usually means that a small spark or ember has breathed its way into fresh fuel, requiring heavy breathing on our parts and an all-too-fresh return to firefighting. Having heard what sounded like crackling popcorn, I lowered my Saturday *Oregonian*, looked up the hill, and saw a small cloud of black smoke suspended atop a swirl of contorting heat waves. A flareup . . . in the damn cheatgrass of all places.

"Hey, it's taking off," I yelled, while grabbing my radio, gloves, and pulaski.

We frantically hosed down some gunnysacks to beat out the flames. By the time we reached the rekindle, it was already blossoming downcanyon, crosscanyon, and upcanyon. Our attempts to dig line, squirt water, and flail our pathetic scraps of burlap were full of sound and fury but signified nothing. After a short but frantic effort, my crew's faces were streaked with sweaty soot over crimson red. I told them to pull back to the engines, take a breather, and there we'd regroup.

Next to hearing the sound of popping corn, the next most sickening realization for a fire supervisor is having to radio for help after all the help went home because the fire was supposedly on life support. I called our dispatcher and requested assistance from Grass Valley and/or any available engines from Prineville. They responded that all federal resources were committed; it would be up to us and the rurals to spend the rest of the day and night chasing fire through wheat fields and Sherman big bluegrass.

At times like this, your universe contracts into safety zones, escape routes, and fire that is eating a hole in the landscape. You do what you can, with the help you have and with the knowledge that except for a distant voice on the other end of the radio, virtually the entire world is unaware that you're engaging a fire. Sometimes fires are small, clinically dead carcasses; other times they're beginning to supernova. Occasionally you meet these expanding blazes with near-anonymous acts of heroism, to save a rancher's house, a stack of alfalfa, or some turn-of-the-century homestead. This is nothing new. During the great fires of 1910 in the northern Rockies, Thaddeus A. Roe, with the help of seven other men, saved Avery, Idaho, from destruction: "The rest of the world didn't know what we were going through. It couldn't and that was the terrible part of it. We might have been the only men in the world for all it mattered. Alone, we were left nothing but our bare hands and the help of our Creator to bring us out alive."[1]

On our virtually anonymous hillside we chased a virtually anonymous fire with rural firefighters whose names we were just learning. At our best, we were trying to save people's property and crops and a small town. At our worst, we were risking our necks for fucking sage and cheatgrass. Anonymity, though, is but thinly veiled infamy: just a few days earlier, a thousand miles to our southeast, an anonymous slope was burning itself into the consciousness of a nation.

By nightfall we were still figuring out where to make our stand. I was riding with Sam Miller, the Sherman County fire chief. When I met Sam for the first time, he reminded me of the actor Sam Elliot: tall, mustache drooping around each side of his mouth almost to his chin, soft-spoken with a down-home accent. Like all firefighters in Sherman County (the feds notwithstanding), Sam was a volunteer; he normally operated heavy equipment for the county road department.

We traveled cross-country in his red "six-pack"—a four-door pickup that can carry six passengers inside—through waist-high CRP (Conservation Reserve Program) grass. I soon learned that Sam likes to drink hot coffee even during the heat of a fire. So he poured me a cup from his green, tanker-sized thermos, most of which cascaded down the front of my shirt and onto my lap as we jolted through little coulees and I wrestled with a cab-width map.

Earlier in the day, after the fire had swept down and then up out of Smith Canyon, it raced through several hundred acres of standing grain, roiling in sheets of flame like burning gasoline.

Since the fire was headed directly for the small farming community of Grass Valley, Sam told his dispatcher to request that the governor invoke the Conflagration Act (an Oregon law that allows local fire agencies to receive firefighting resources from across the state, compensated by the state). By the next morning, fire engines from Portland, Corvallis, Molalla, Bend, Redmond, The Dalles, and all parts in between would be pouring into Grass Valley. In the meantime, we had our gloved hands and either luck or help from the Creator to make sure Grass Valley didn't turn to ash.

A one-lane dirt road, chewed to the consistency of brown talcum, was the only fuel-break between the fire to the west and 640 acres of wheat that butted up against the windward side of Grass Valley to our east. Simply put, a fuel-break, control-line, or fire-line is some area that won't burn, a point at which you hope to stop a fire. It could be a strip of ground scraped to mineral soil—that is, bare dirt. It could also be a river, a verdant meadow, or a rockslide. How wide it needs to be to stop a fire depends on how hot the fire is burning. And if your fire is burning intense and moving fast, it's often better to set a "backfire" than allow the main fire to hit your fuel-break full force.

Until I began fighting fire, the concept of backfiring was a mystery: What's the point in starting more fire than you already have? Moreover, if a stiff wind is driving a grass fire toward your strip of bare dirt, won't any fire you set likewise jump your line unfettered? Well, not necessarily. All fires will burn against the wind, though much slower than their downwind fronts. Plus, as the main fire approaches your location, its appetite for oxygen causes air to rush toward itself. Hence, by setting a controlled backfire, you're trying to increase the width of your fuel-break by eliminating vegetation (fuel) in advance of the main fire—taking advantage of a fire's ability to both back against the prevailing wind and cause its own backdraft. That is, in theory. If you wait too long to set your backfire, you'll fail to create a wide enough buffer of black, and the main fire will jump your line; if winds are brisk, your backfire might extend its flames over your fire-line, "spotting" into fresh fuel and continuing cross-country, leaving nothing but a strip of mineral soil bracketed by smoldering grass and bruised egos.

I hoped that we could organize a backfire from the road and at least herd the fire around Grass Valley. However, for a county that is a good forty miles from the nearest live bear, many of the ranchers and farmers along our strip of brown talcum had obviously taken Smokey's words to heart and wanted nothing to do with laying down more fire. For them, the only logical, and manly, way to fight fire was head-on. By the time all the parties who needed to agree had agreed to fight fire with fire, it was too late. Within minutes, flames would be reaching across the rusted barbed wire on one side of the road to meet kindling-dry fence-posts, more rusted barbed wire, and 640 acres of cured winter wheat on the other.

By Sherman County standards, my crew must have seemed like wimps, but there'd been enough death for one week. I told Sam that this is where we parted company. Someone needed to be at Grass Valley if (and, in my mind, when) the fire crossed the road. Plus, in firefighter parlance, the road had become one big clusterfuck—bumper-to-bumper fire trucks, flatbed farm rigs, cowdogs, cowboy hats, weedsprayers, and whining ATVs and children. My two engines staged at the west edge of Grass Valley, where I requested state police assistance for traffic control. We watched for the inevitable orange glow that would soon crest the hill, brighten like a sunset over Mount Hood to the west, then flood the backyards of town.

Over the radio, Sam Miller's voice boomed through the darkness: "Get ready boys, you're looking down the throat of Old Man Devil, and here he comes."

I can only imagine the firefight that followed along that thin dirt road. Manly men grappling with fire—hoses wildly squirting into a blistering curtain of flame as it hit the road and arched over Super Dutys and Korean-era duce-and-a-halfs. The yelling: "Back those rigs up." "Get up here, we got a spot." Tires spinning in the powdery ditches, red lights rotating atop cabs submerged in dust and smoke. It would have been a sight to see, though I'm glad I didn't.

The expected glow never came; their heroics were successful. For the night, Grass Valley was safe. It's a wonder some of their asses weren't fried. I half expected a call for medical help from Sam or one of his assistants. Thankfully, it didn't come, but if it had, I wouldn't have been surprised. Never mind that in moments of calm reflection even the ranchers along the dirt county road wouldn't gamble their lives for bunchgrass and sage, even a section of wheat. However, when a fire is on the horizon and something that you value is about to be incinerated, your world collapses into categories of instinct buttressed by optimism, and sometimes foolishness. You forget that your body is 60 percent water, waiting to boil. You forget that even though no one in recent memory has died fighting grass fires in Sherman County, lots of people have died in lots of counties just like Sherman.

...

Death inhabits the West. Abstractly, you might look for it in disease and ethnic "cleansing," in torrents of water or ice, or within the suffocating confines of collapsing tunnels. Concretely, call it the Trail of Tears or Wounded Knee, the Great Flood of Heppner, Oregon, or the Sunshine Mine disaster. And then there is fire.

Death by fire is nothing new. Whether trying to save something of value or trying to save something that you just think is valuable, the possibility always exists for little misjudgments to supernova into big tragedies (or, as Norman Maclean put it regarding the Mann Gulch fire, for "little screwups" to fit "together tighter and tighter until all became one and the same thing—the fateful blowup").[2] In fact, for as long as humans have called North America home there have been misjudgments—misjudgments tucked away in box canyons or prairies that, after the firefront had passed, left nothing but white-hot buffalo chips, smoldering buckskin, and a few smoke-stained arrowheads.

In 1832, the explorer and artist George Catlin wrote about the dangers associated with grass fires:

There is yet another character of burning prairies . . . the war, or hell of fires! where the grass is seven or eight feet high . . . and the flames are driven forward by the hurricanes, which often sweep over the vast prairies of this denuded country. There are many of these meadows on the Missouri, and the Platte, and the Arkansas, of many miles in breadth, which are perfectly level, with waving grass, so high, that we are obliged to stand erect in our stirrups, in order to look over its waving tops, as we are riding through it. The fire in these, before such a wind, travels at an immense and frightful rate, and often destroys, on their fleetest horses, parties of Indians, who are so unlucky as to be overtaken by it.[3]

All the same reasons people die fighting fires today would have applied prior to the age of organized fire suppression: heat, fuel, and oxygen were necessary to ignite a fire; weather, topography, and fuel characteristics would then determine how the fire burned. And anytime, for whatever reason, people (or any animals, for that matter) got in the way of a fire—due to misjudging fire speed, wind speed, or what constituted a sufficient buffer around one's village—death and injury were real possibilities.

Potentially, just about any piece of the western landscape holds death. Modern fatality sites attract those wanting to see where human judgments and the fire triangle converged to forge tragedy. I too have walked upon such pieces of ground, hallowed ground, to see what combination of factors led to death. But from the standpoint of sheer possibility, there is a fine line between anonymity and infamy. Mythic names such as Setzer Creek, Blackwater, Mann Gulch, Inaja, Cart Creek, Rattlesnake,

Loop, South Canyon, Thirtymile, and sundry others emblazoned on bronze tablets and granite crosses are no different from thousands, even millions, of other named and unnamed spots hemmed in by township, range, and section lines. All are free of death for a time, but certainly not immune. Many testify to people getting in the way of fire, and our desire that they be there to keep fire from getting in our way.

Some authors have argued for reducing fuel loadings (that is, the amount of vegetation per unit area) in the West, with one of the justifications being that in presettlement landscapes fuels would have been thinned by more frequent—though lower-intensity—fires. No doubt there is truth in this, even if many ignitions came from the hands of North America's first peoples. Reducing fuel, or modifying the flammability of fuel through changing the composition and structure of vegetation, is seen as ecologically good, an act of restoration. Again, this holds truth, though it cannot be generalized. But besides the ecological argument for fuel reduction, there is a safety argument—that the buildup of fuels is leading to larger, more dangerous fires, evidenced in increasing numbers of fatalities. However, this contention ignores the fact that fires have always had the potential to become large and deadly.

No matter how light the fuels, when weather conditions were right, fires played over thousands of acres. Even viewed from the truncated view of two centuries, the currently popular—and politically evocative—assertion that fires are getting bigger and more dangerous is astounding, and simply inaccurate. For instance, the author Richard Manning writes that "by the standards of the day, it [Mann Gulch] was a big fire, ultimately about 4,500 acres. Subsequent drought cycles have eroded those standards. Now a big fire is like the 250,000-acre blaze in 1988 that burned just a few miles from Mann Gulch"—the implication being that fire suppression begat fuel buildups, which in turn begat larger fires.[4] But look for a moment to the past:

Miramichi fire (Maine), 1825: 3,000,000 acres, 160 deaths.
Silverton fire (Oregon), 1865: 1,000,000 acres.
Peshtigo fire (Wisconsin), 1871: 1,280,000 acres, 1,500 deaths.
Hinckley fire (Minnesota), 1894: 160,000 acres, 418 deaths.
Northern Rockies (Idaho and Montana), 1910: 3,000,000
    acres, 85 deaths.[5]

Hardly innocuous. True, fire statistics show a general downward trend in burned acreage in the western United States throughout the twentieth century that might be at least partially attributable to organized fire suppression—although the trend began to reverse in the late 1980s. But the fact that such expansive, pre-fire-suppression-era blazes occurred argues against simple generalizations that today's burned acreages are somehow unprecedented. By some estimates, 18 to 25 million acres may have burned annually in the western United States prior to 1900, nearly four times as much as what burned in the year 2000, a reputed large-acreage fire year.[6]

Moreover, like the fire-behavior triune of fuel, weather, and topography, every new firefighter is taught the common denominators of tragedy fires—pithy nuggets such as:

1. Most incidents happen on smaller fires or on isolated sections of larger fires.
2. Flareups generally occur in deceptively light fuels.
3. Most fires are innocent in appearance before unexpected shifts in wind direction.
4. Fires respond to large- and small-scale topographic conditions.

Undoubtedly, where fires have been suppressed for decades, fuel buildups may contribute to hotter fires, more difficult to suppress. Yet these are typically not the most dangerous, for when a fire is erupting in a thermonuclear-like plume, personnel are often (though not always) far removed from the flames, burning up rolls of Kodachrome. It's when they are up close, at a point in the fire's history where it looks like it isn't doing much—merely snaking through light grass and tinder—that people get caught off guard. That's where death lurks, where it potentially lurked just north of Smith Canyon.

• • •

The next couple of days in Grass Valley were a blur. The first day and a half of the Smith Canyon fire, I served as a joint incident commander with Sam Miller. Eventually, as the fire continued to expand and more firefighting resources poured into town, district management reassigned me to oversee fire "operations" (that is, to directly supervise suppression efforts). Management is always a little edgy when an escaped fire isn't caught by the next morning; consequently, more black acres plus increased public scrutiny equated to a new job for Mr. Strohmaier.

We now had two helicopters working the fire, a Bell Jet Ranger and an old snub-nosed Sikorsky. Eventually we would have a third helicopter with a heli-rappel crew out of John Day. Not that we needed rappellers to descend through the six-foot canopy of sagebrush, but we needed a helicopter and people, and they were some of the only reinforcements available.

The ranchers and farmers I've worked with over the years are a common-sense lot. Just grab your irrigation shovel, maybe a gunnysack or old pair of Levis that you've soaked with water, and bail off the canyon rim to wherever there is smoke. Knock the fire down, turn over the cow pies, jab around where there are flames, then climb back out of the canyon to your pickup or idling combine and a six-pack of Bud. If the fire rekindles, repeat the process. As a federal firefighter, you're taught always to wear personal protective gear, like hardhats and Nomex, always to have an escape route to a safety zone in which you can calmly ride out the fire in case of a blowup, and always to carry a fire shelter (an aluminum-foil-like tent) in which to hunker if your escape routes are cut off or you misjudge the viability of your safety zone. But looking at these farmers and ranchers sometimes makes me wonder why I take such precautions. They herringbone their way across the bunchgrass slopes in their Tony Lamas; the mother-of-pearl buttons on their cotton-poly-blend shirts sparkle in the sun; baseball caps or Stetsons protect their noggins. Gloves are optional. No backpacks or fire shelters. No drinking water. Can of Copenhagen in the back pocket. Lucky bastards, is all I can say.

Common sense resembled chaos on the evening of the third full day of the incident. A group of farmers, impatient with the plan to backfire from roads and bulldozer lines, dove off into the canyon near the head of the fire, which is akin to cleaning a chimney with a fire blazing in the stove below. Not wise. There were radio reports of trapped firefighters. I told the BLM helitack (helicopter-attack) foreman to launch our ship in the direction of the alleged entrapment with the Bambi bucket (a plastic, collapsible water bucket dangling from a cable beneath the helicopter) and do what he could to find the firefighters and cool them off. I rounded up an ambulance crew and had them stand by in the event there were injuries.

Backfiring was suspended. Roads became plugged with huge city fire engines, usually reserved for fighting house fires and virtually all two-wheel drive. We'd later discover that a group of "eight farmers and a bartender" descended into the canyon to take matters into their own hands. As one farmer put it, "We've been up here for four days . . . we want to get in and put the damn thing out. It was about time someone [read: other than the feds] got in there and did something."[7] Well, they did something all right: they paralyzed the overall fire effort as we mounted a rescue. Our district manager, one hundred miles away, heard the disturbing radio traffic and took it upon himself to divert a retardant plane from a fire near John Day to our location. When the pink-bellied DC-6 arrived west of Grass Valley, it painted a fallow field red, missing the fire completely. The pilots might as well have tossed a $6,000 wad of cash out the window on a flyby.

Amazingly, the farmers actually did "put a stop on the fire," and they were no worse for the wear, except for breathing too much smoke and suffering slight dehydration. After the fact, we were able to laugh at the thought of the eight farmers attacking the head, or at least the most active flank, of the fire, their bar-towel-snapping sidekick bringing up the rear. At the time, though, it made me mad as hell, for they could have got themselves killed. It reminds me of a passage written by the nineteenth-century Danish philosopher and theologian Søren Kierkegaard:

> Hardly is the cry of "Fire!" heard before a crowd of people rush to the spot, nice, cordial, sympathetic, helpful people, one has a pitcher, another a basin, the third a squirt, etc., all of them nice, cordial, sympathetic, helpful people, so eager to help put out the fire.
>
> But what says the Fire Chief? The Fire Chief, he says—yes, generally the Fire Chief is a very pleasant and polite man; but at a fire he is what one calls coarse-mouthed—he says, or rather he bawls, "Oh, go to hell with all your pitchers and squirts. . . . And when some policemen arrive he says to them, "Rid me of these damn people with their pitchers and squirts; and if they won't yield to fair words, smear them a few over the back, so that we may be free of them and get down to work."[8]

If only it were so.

In the midst of the confusion, and lacking police to smear anyone over the back, I pulled all BLM resources back to Grass Valley to regroup and figure out how to organize the free-for-all. Our incident command post was in the Grass Valley fire hall, a metal, three-bay building with an office that doubled as city hall. The dance that should have taken place Saturday night had been canceled, but the Henry Weinhard's Brewery truck still sat in the first bay, Private Reserve beer going flat.

It was apparent that the parties responsible for managing the fire—BLM, rural fire departments, state fire marshal's office, and private landowners—needed to talk and stop second-guessing each other. The next time an impromptu posse of free agents "got in there and did something," they might be stirring the coals for their own barbecue.

While waiting for the meeting to begin, I stood in the cramped little office of the firehall watching a TV monitor that hung from the ceiling in one corner of the room. The evening news was playing. There I stood in my yellow, sweat-stained Nomex shirt —amidst the bickering, drifting cigarette smoke, rumors of unaccounted for civilian firefighters, and complaints about the lazy BLM—watching flag-draped caskets carried off an old, silver DC-3 embossed with the words "U.S. Forest Service." Biting my lip, I tried to fight off tears.

Only a handful of others in the room watched the coverage. But I wanted them all to watch. Weren't they aware that a number of our kin were coming home? Couldn't people just shut up for a minute and put what we were doing in perspective?

Several days earlier, these ones, now sealed in caskets and draped with American flags, were cutting brush and digging line and breathing smoke . . . like us. Several days earlier they were trying to contain a fire that didn't look particularly threatening; it was just a big pain in the ass. However, only a few hours after being dropped off by a helicopter on an obscure finger ridge of Storm King Mountain, nine Prineville firefighters would be dead, never to engage the fires of summer again. And other towns—radiating out from points like Missoula, McCall, Grand Junction, and Glenwood Springs—would soon be reeling from the news of firefighters killed in action.

For a few minutes, the margins of my universe collapsed to the size of a small TV screen suspended in the corner of a small room.

The meeting convened. I cleared my throat but still had difficulty speaking through the lingering mist of tarmac and caskets and grieving families. I told the group that we'd lost too many firefighters that week. I can't remember what else I said, probably something like, "No chunk of ground is worth getting killed over," or, "We've got to maintain order and communications."

In the end, eight farmers and a bartender were the heroes. Heroes or not, my crew was alive—and in the world of fire, being alive counts for something.

• • •

On July 14 the Smith Canyon fire was controlled. I returned home to Prineville, a place showing marks of a more permanent homecoming. On the grassy median on the west end of town rose a circle of American flags, usually only present on the Fourth of July or Memorial Day. In front of the Crook County Courthouse were nine more flags, planted in a row. At night they were illumined by floodlamps. When I first saw their colors against the backlit stone courthouse, a chill spasmed through my body. The flags were stark, palpably close reminders that fighting fire is damned serious business.

A month later my wife and I were en route to New Haven, Connecticut, where we were both graduate students. We liked to take a new route each time we traversed the continent. This time the most logical path led a thousand miles to our southeast. We picked up Interstate 70 near Green River, Utah, then traveled east into Colorado, through Grand Junction, to the base of Storm King Mountain. Between BLM contour maps and images soldered into my memory from TV news footage, we easily located the exposed red dirt and ashy gray slopes of the burn. We exited the freeway at Canyon Creek Estates, where faded purple ribbons fluttered from mailboxes and fences.

Wanting to make it to Denver by evening, we had only enough time for a quick hike to the fatality site. In my backpack I carried the official investigative report of the fire, which contained a map of the fire area; however, the aerial news clips of nine yellow tarps dotting a moonscaped slope were still too clear in my mind for me to need prompting.

It took an hour and a half to reach ground zero—hiking cross-country through punky dry juniper, sage, piñon pine, and Gambel oak, then through soft gray ash and blackened oak skeletons.

Only six weeks after the fire, new shoots of Gambel oak—already six inches tall—poked out of the hillside. Amidst the oak shoots were steel spikes, also about six inches tall. Attached to the spikes were small brass tags stamped with the letters "FF" (for "firefighter") and the numbers 1 through 12. Not much else identified this as the spot where twelve young men and women were last alive, though there were clues: a basket of crunchy yellow wildflowers, a few purple ribbons hanging from a burnt juniper snag, churned-up ground where family members and investigators had milled around since early July. I didn't have time to locate the markers for the two Grand Junction helitack crew members who died near the head of a rocky draw, numbers 13 and 14. I did find the fire's point of origin, where someone had planted a flag that flew at half-staff. I found the original fireline that was overrun when the dry cold front passed over the fire on the afternoon of July 6, fifty-mile-per-hour winds mixing gases and smoke into a cauliflower-shaped plume. And I found the ridge where a number of smokejumpers hunkered in their fire shelters until the blowup subsided.

Four years later I returned to Storm King Mountain. In the meantime, there would be more memorial services, a continuing investigation and federal fire management review, and time to grieve and remember and meditate on why the hell we fight fire where within a month's time Gambel oak will grow to the height of steel spikes.

• • •

[63]

"We will not forget" became the motto for the towns of Prineville and Glenwood Springs once the news of fatalities was announced. But in thinking about other fatality fires, I'm reminded that the half-life of remembered tragedy is directly related to one's proximity to the world of firefighting, or personal attachment to those extinguishing a world on fire. Memories fade. After a generation or two, old wounds from old fires have sealed over, or at least filled in with duff and time, so that only a few historians, fire buffs, or friends and family of the deceased remember their flames. What had been a well-trodden path to the ground upon which firefighters sucked in their last breaths becomes faded and overgrown. To find even a few sparks of remembered grief requires a lot of cold-trailing. Some of my cold-trailing led me to the Bitterroot Mountains of eastern Idaho.

Joe Halm wrote that "the great sacrifice of human life" in the 1910 fires "can never be replaced or forgotten." In theory, he's right. In reality, the two monuments in Nine Mile Cemetery in Wallace, Idaho, speak otherwise. To find them, all I had to go by were old photos and the words of a Forest Service ranger, Edward Pulaski: "Suitable headstones with bronze tablets were erected over as many of these 'heroes of peace' as could be traced, for they died as truly in the service of their country as did those on Flanders' poppy-covered fields."[9] After two trips to the thickly wooded cemetery, I finally found both memorials.

One memorial sits at the top edge of the cemetery, in the "Grand Mound Section." The other, a little lower on the hill in the "Catholic Section," is wedged between lichen-encrusted headstones and large ponderosa pines. With the exception of different names on each, the memorials are identical: a five-foot-tall pillar of mortared river rock in front of which sits a ten-foot-wide flower bed, also walled-in by mortared rock. A bronze tablet is mounted on each pillar. An old U.S. Forest Service file photo from the Northern Region office shows the tablets crisp and bright. Today they're chalky green. On each tablet is a raised seal of the U.S. Forest Service, below which are the names of the men buried in that plot and the simple inscription: "Died Fighting Forest Fires, August 20, 1910."

The Catholic Section plaque lists five men. The first simply says "Unidentified Man." In a barely known cemetery, wildland firefighters also have their tomb of the unknown. He was probably some vagrant or unemployed miner or lumberjack from Butte or Missoula or Spokane, picked up and conscripted into service by a Forest Service employee. Toward the end, before being overtaken by one of this century's most deadly firestorms for firefighting personnel, he was no doubt scared as hell. By the looks of the weedy flower beds in front of each monument, they're only sporadically maintained, if at all. Or maybe flowers no longer flourish under the deep shade of the now-towering trees. Inset in the mortar at the top of each pillar is a small metal tube. The old photos show that, at one time, small flags were planted in the tubes. Now they're filled with rainwater and pine needles.

We will not forget.

There's another firefighter memorial in Saint Maries, Idaho. Fifty-seven granite headstones form concentric circles around a solid stone monument and a white, peeling flagpole. On each small headstone is engraved the name of a firefighter, the name of a fire, and a date. Setzer Creek, Big Creek, Clark Fork, Noxon. August 20. The times that my wife and I have visited there, we've made a point to walk the circles and read each name, the name of a person who died trying to protect something that people valued. And as with the unidentified man in the Nine Mile Cemetery, some of the headstones say "unknown."

We will not forget.

In all, seventy-eight firefighters and seven civilians died during that wind-induced firestorm on August 20 and 21 of 1910. Like firebrands before a convection column, the casualties spread over four national forests—Saint Joe, Coeur d'Alene, Cabinet, Pend Oreille. Within those forests many crews suffered losses, including the crews of Pulaski, Bell, Rock, Debbit, Hollingshead, Danielson, Taylor, and other foremen. The towns of Taft, DeBorgia, Haugin, and Tuscor collapsed in smoking ruins. Much of Wallace was razed. It's hard to imagine the collective trauma of that many deaths, within two days, in the small communities of Idaho and Montana. If that many deaths occurred today from fire, wildland fire agencies would be reviewing their programs for decades. But the Forest Service was young, as was its understanding of fire behavior.

A lot has changed since 1910. The first snows of winter were just dusting the Bitterroots that year when F. A. Silcox, assistant District 1 forester, confidently wrote that "there is not the slightest doubt but that with an adequate trail, lookout, and telephone system, and a sufficient equipment of tools, the fires [of the future] can be controlled."[10] Yes, we built the trails, lookouts, telephone lines, and tool caches, plus a small air force and an infrastructure that Silcox couldn't even imagine. We also controlled thousands of fires throughout the West.

But some things haven't changed. When the time is right, fires will burn regardless of our technology. We gave up on trying to control lightning. People still get in the way of fires, make little and big mistakes, misjudge the speed of advancing flame fronts, take foolish risks, and forget that their bodies are mainly water that boils at 212 degrees Fahrenheit. We don't want to forget the past, but we do. Moreover, every decade of the twentieth century confirms that no multiplication of safety rules will remove death from the margins of fires:

1910, Northern Rockies	78 firefighters
1933, Griffith Park	25 firefighters
1937, Blackwater	15 firefighters
1943, Hauser Creek	11 firefighters
1949, Mann Gulch	13 firefighters
1953, Rattlesnake	15 firefighters
1956, Inaja	11 firefighters
1966, Loop	12 firefighters
1976, Battlement Creek	3 firefighters

1990, Dude	6 firefighters
1994, South Canyon	14 firefighters
2001, Thirtymile	4 firefighters

Between each line are many other fires and casualties. In all, be-tween 1910 and 1996 nearly 700 firefighters died on wildfires in the United States.[11] Since then, the tally has continued to rise. Numerically, 700-plus deaths may pale before other sacrifices to public service and losses of life in America; they're losses, none-theless. They're losses that need remembering. And many of them occurred under the sun beyond the 100th meridian.

So fires have always had the potential to grow large; under the right circumstances, with the right winds, they can grow into conflagrations. Fires have always claimed lives, too, doing so at a fairly predictable pace across the decades of the twentieth cen-tury. There's no reason to believe that we are moving toward a state of evolutionary fitness with regard to fire. We don't shed our limbs. We don't release seed from fire-stiffened carcasses. Yet firefighters continue to die. The best we can do is to remember, to remember the lungs that breathed their last at the countless margins separating green from black, to remember what didn't work in the past and what might work in the future.

Death inhabits the West: in our memories, however faint; in the afterglow of barely cool ashes; and in the manifold possibili-ties of tragedy in virtually every mountain range and valley. Over the last century and a half we've created all manner of ways to die or be killed. And notwithstanding our creativity in purposely killing one another, many of these possibilities for death were a function of risk. Because we valued gold and silver and coal, we burrowed into the ground only to have the ground shift or the air explode, sealing life where life is normally absent. A farm tractor slips in steep, powdery loam, and the law of gravity inverts its mass upon the driver. Accidental, tragic, all worthy of mourning. Yet, rightly or wrongly, there is something different about death by fire. Fire is primal, very ancient though seasonally reborn. We may contribute to the conditions that allow fires to burn (like patterns of settlement and agriculture that break up fuel continuity), but fire has burned for millions of years, with all terrestrial life sharing the possibility and reality of death in its wake. Fire reminds us of judgment. It's not a void; it's a presence—a presence that moves through space and time. Fire is mysterious, for the flames speak to the hidden potential of matter, the potential for change: hot, lethal change. Lethal because we get in its way. And death by fire, while suppressing fire, is often viewed as public service, transmuting accident into sacrifice. But is this view correct? Moreover, even if *sacrifice* is the correct word to describe the deaths of firefighters, are all the sacrifices for the sake of extinguishing fire for naught?

Regardless of the era, the words of eulogy for fire's casualties are remarkably similar, even if our ideas about wildfire have changed. Edward Pulaski compared the sacrifices of fallen firefighters to those who died on "Flanders' poppy-covered fields" during World War I. One writer, reflecting on the fires of 1910, stated that "the war, brief as it was, had all the elements that at-

[69]

tend the life and death struggles of nations."[12] The analogy works to a point, then breaks down. For unlike the conflicts between nations, the alleged enemy—fire—has burned without will or consciousness from time immemorial. Our problem is, we get in its way; we become fuel. Nevertheless, to the extent that fire burns where we don't want it to burn, that we shove and coerce it to wilt into smoldering abeyance, that it requires armies of people to herd it between subdivisions and mountain ranges, that it consumes human lives and human property, and that fighting fire is seen as a public service, it's *like* war. And maybe this warlikeness is another reason why death by fire, while fighting fire, seems different from other ways to die as part of one's work.

On August 20, 1939, Paul R. Greever, an American Legion post commander and former congressman, gave the dedication address for the Blackwater Memorial, located between Cody, Wyoming, and Yellowstone National Park:

Two years ago today a forest fire started on the watershed of Blackwater Creek, to the south of this site. A call for fire fighters went out and these young men, together with their comrades, set out to extinguish the fire. These boys for hours fought the raging blaze. They cut timber, and fought the fire in every way known; cut, bruised and injured by fierce scorching blasts as the walls of fire closed in upon them. Some were suffocated, some were burned. . . .

. . . . These young men whom we honor today are entitled to the same honor for their sacrifice as are those of our comrades who died upon the battlefield, because they, too, sacrificed themselves upon the altar of public duty. . . .

We cannot understand why these things should be. We cannot understand why a young life, in the full exuberance of youth, with the promise of a happy career, should thus be snatched away, but our comfort lies in our belief in immortality. We cannot understand why these young lives should be apparently wasted, but we must know they are not wasted. We know that their example alone is sufficient, even without this beautiful monument, to give them a place in the hearts of all who knew of their sacrifice.[13]

Platitudes? Well, maybe partially. Mainly, though, they're words reflecting deep loss—loss that is not without meaning—loss that is supreme, though for a cause. The painful losses inscribed in black granite on the Mall in Washington, D.C., make me wonder whether the trail of tears sprinkled amidst the ashes of western wildfires has often been a waste. Has the battle against wildfire been a tragic police action against nature, a pursuit of lofty ideals that in the end is unworkable, flawed because we live in a world that has evolved to burn? Maybe so, but not always.

From the 1910 Bitterroot fires to Blackwater to Mann Gulch to South Canyon, eulogies echo the same themes of sacrifice and courage, even tragedy. While a nauseating ennui has permeated much of our culture—a deconstructionist relativism that admits catastrophe but no tragedy—for most in the West who have brushed up against fire and death, the word *tragedy* still makes sense, even if it lacks the haughty precision of academia.

• • •

Norman Maclean struggled to transform the deaths of thirteen firefighters from catastrophe into tragedy. *Young Men and Fire* is a testament to that quest, undertaken largely during the twilight of his life.[14]

Philosophers often talk of "possible worlds"—an infinite number of imagined universes or states of affairs. Given different initial conditions in our own world, different decisions on the part of creatures with free will (namely us), or a totally different universe (so long as nothing in it violates the logician's chestnut of noncontradiction), you end up with a "possible," though not necessarily actual, world. The world we live in is both possible and actual. In a sense Maclean envisioned the possible world that he could have lived if he had stayed in Montana rather than joining the faculty of the University of Chicago. His story of the Mann Gulch fire brings his scholarly life as a classicist and storyteller to bear on the world he might have lived but didn't, the world that others lived but whose stories went untold. In his attempt to tell this story of fire and young smokejumpers he uses old forms to chink gaps in a partially outlined catastrophe.

The first form is biblical. The parallels between Maclean and the author of Ecclesiastes are hard to miss.
Maclean:

> I, an old man, have written this fire report. Among other things, it was important to me, as an exercise for old age, to enlarge my knowledge and spirit so I could accompany young men whose lives I might have lived on their way to death. I have climbed where they climbed, and in my time I have fought fire and inquired into its nature. In addition, I have lived to get a better understanding of myself and those close to me, many of them now dead.[15]

Ecclesiastes:

> I the Preacher have been king over Israel in Jerusalem. And I applied my mind to seek and to search out by wisdom all that is done under heaven; it is an unhappy business that God has given to the sons of men to be busy with. I have seen everything that is done under the sun; and behold, all is vanity and a striving after wind.
>
> . . .
>
> And I applied my mind to know wisdom and to know madness and folly. I perceived that this also is but a striving after wind.[16]

But while the Preacher finds nothing new under the sun—from interminable natural cycles that amount to vanity, to pointless effort that lands both rich and poor moldering in the same cold graves of Sheol—Maclean struggles to find some meaning in death, if only the meaning present in death explained.

The second form is classical. Most people use *tragedy* to mean an unfortunate event, something that shouldn't have occurred, like someone dying before his or her time. But "classical" tragedy is defined as serious dramatic art with a beginning, middle, and end "in which a great person of noble stature is seen inexorably to fall from a state of happiness to a state of undeserved suffering or misery."[17] This noble person falls into misfortune due to "some error in judgment," not due to inexplicable events.[18] In that sense, its hard to imagine the death of a Butte alcoholic or a teenage smokejumper as being tragic.

However, Maclean means something else, yet related—something closer to how we commonly use the term, though a little

[73]

more. "This tragedy [in Mann Gulch] is not a classical tragedy of a monumental individual crossing the sword of his will with the sword of destiny. It is a tragedy of a crew, its flaws and grandeurs largely those of Smokejumpers near the beginning of their history."[19] Catastrophe remains a gaping wound, a mystery, inexplicable and forever inconsolable. What is truly catastrophic is to suffer and die for no reason. To empathize is a step toward explaining, and for Maclean, explanation is key. To explain a thing is to move terror toward tragedy. And here I'll let Maclean speak for himself:

> Although young men died like squirrels in Mann Gulch, the Mann Gulch fire should not end there, smoke drifting away and leaving terror without consolation of explanation, and controversy without lasting settlement. Probably most catastrophes end this way without an ending, the dead not even knowing how they died but "still alertly erect in fear and wonder," those who loved them forever questioning "this unnecessary death," and the rest of us tiring of this inconsolable catastrophe and turning to the next one. This [Mann Gulch fire] is a catastrophe that we hope will not end where it began; it might go on and become a story. It will not have to be made up—that is all-important to us—but we do have to know in what odd places to look for missing parts of a story about a wildfire and of course have to know a story and a wildfire when we see one. So this story is a test of its own belief—that in this cockeyed world there are shapes and designs, if only we have some curiosity, training, and compassion and take care not to lie or be sentimental.[20]

Maclean cobbles tragedy out of his blistering summer hikes into Mann Gulch, out of conversations with the two remaining survivors of the fire and trips to the Forest Service fire lab in Missoula to understand the chemistry of a fire blowup, and in his struggle to understand the decisions that firefighters made as their world became fire. These were firefighters who had stories of their own that, for eleven, ended abruptly on August 5, 1949, and for two more ended the next day in a Helena hospital. For those who survived the fire or brushed up against the terror of those who didn't, August 5 would be inscribed on their lives until they, too, met death. Historic, scientific, personal: all of these stories, for Maclean, help fill in the story of Mann revealing patterns in the inchoate, moving catastrophe toward tragedy. Although we live in a universe that remains untamed, it is not necessarily chaotic or meaningless: "But we should be prepared for the possibility, even if we are going to accompany modern firefighters into Mann Gulch, that the terror of the universe has not yet fossilized and the universe has not run out of blowups. Yet we should also go on wondering if there is not some shape, form, design as of artistry in this universe we are entering that is composed of catastrophes and missing parts."[21]

Here is where the loss of fire runs headlong into the loss of life: Is there room for tragedy in a world that always has burned and should continue to burn? Do the facts of fire ecology obviate human ecology and compassion and render a filled-in story nothing more than a glorified catastrophe? Can we navigate between these two cairns?

Richard Manning admits that, as literature, *Young Men and Fire* succeeds. Nevertheless, according to Manning, "as an account of nature it is myopic and negligently incomplete." He lambastes Maclean for demonizing fire: "It is evil. It is a monster. It is death generalized to the point that by the end of the book it is transformed to nuclear fire, in that 'it looked much like an atomic explosion in Nevada on its cancerous way to Utah.'"[22] True, Maclean does employ similes and metaphors, and to the extent that he actually demonizes fire, he is ecologically culpable and deserves criticism.

But on my reading, Maclean has primarily embarked upon what he calls a "journey of compassion."[23] Moreover, he does note that Indians set fire to improve rangeland and that positive ecological effects result from wildfire (which is more than many an early-twentieth-century forester could croak out).[24] At least minimally, then, alongside metaphors that suggest otherwise, he acknowledged a positive side to fire. Still, Maclean's story of Mann Gulch is largely concerned with something else, and to read it as a primer in fire ecology is itself "myopic and negligently incomplete." This "something else" is an important counterbalance to the ecological glad game.

What do you tell family members of those who died like squirrels in Mann Gulch, in Blackwater Canyon, or on Storm King Mountain? Do you respond like Job's friends—Eliphaz, Bildad, and Zophar—who assumed that suffering must instruct, show fault, or reflect blame or impiety? After all, it's our own damn fault for getting in the way of a going fire. Do you respond that since a police action against nature is rarely justified, those act-ing as police are not worthy of mourning? Do all the ecological goods of fire dissolve the cultural harms it sometimes inflicts?

Fire in the West is not an either/or proposition. Fire can be both ecologically good and culturally bad, simultaneously. It can be fought with the best of intentions, even if myopic. It's possible to both remember those who died along its margins and envision how we want those margins to burn in the future. Speaking truth requires all of these, and more. For the ecological Pollyanna, tragedy diminishes before a smile superimposed on the yin and yang of a beautifully complex universe. However, the ecological losses associated with the loss of fire must be viewed together with the cultural and deeply personal losses fire (and its loss) brings—to the things we love, to the people we love.

Humans have long been able to make the best of bad situations. Maybe I only exist today because my distant relatives in the genus *Homo*, on some distant African savanna, suffered enough brutal ends and struggles against a changing climate to, ever so slowly, evolve into *sapiens*. Sweet fortuity . . . in retrospect. We've learned lessons from the deaths of firefighters who breathed their last on anonymous hills in little-known regions of the West. However, I can't say we're better off because of their deaths. How many deaths must be offered up on the altar of remorse before we learn some lesson or other about how to better live in a world that always has, always will, and, indeed, should burn? Might we learn lessons without flag-draped caskets? I think so, if we can just remember.

• • •

While the South Canyon fire still burned, I began collecting newspaper clippings, government press releases, really anything that had to do with the fire. Today, a decade after the ashes cooled, I still add to these items, now bound in a green three-ring binder: "Reunion at Redmond," "Saying Farewell to the Nine," a program for the Prineville Wildland Firefighters Monument dedication, a map of Storm King Mountain. A blue ribbon remains pinned to the fabric inside my pickup behind the rearview mirror. These are all links to my past, and reminders of the potential costs of engaging fires in the future.

In 1949 Bob Jansson was the ranger for the Canyon Ferry District of the Helena National Forest. His district encompassed the Gates of the Mountains Wild Area (today's Gates of the Mountains Wilderness), which held Mann Gulch. In an unpublished autobiography, Lois Jansson, Bob's wife, reflects on the aftermath of the Mann Gulch Fire for her family. For example, their son Roger "was less than a year old when our first serious troubles began, and I have always felt regret that we lost so much of the enjoyment we should all have had in his first year. There is no baby book of his cute sayings, no collection of baby pictures, only a scrapbook full of newspaper clippings of tragedy."[25]

Should smokejumpers have been dropped into a tinder-dry gulch to extinguish a fire in a roadless area that had hosted fires for millennia? Maybe not. If they had gotten there earlier and had stopped the fire, would the canyon have eventually burned? Probably so. But that's not how history played out, and within thirty minutes the entire gulch burned out, along with thirteen

[78]

lives and the hopes and dreams of many more. Even though Ranger Jansson survived—escaping through spotfires to the cool waters of the Missouri before a torrent of flame defied gravity and flowed upgulch—he was forever catfaced by the inferno, especially from the rescue effort later that night:

> Bob came home Sunday afternoon for a twenty-four hour rest, so tired and unstrung he hardly seemed like the husband and father we knew. I knew the children were frightened and I couldn't do much for them because I was frightened, too. His feet were in terrible shape, swollen so that it was very hard to get his boots off, and the socks—glued on by running blisters, had to be soaked off in the bathtub. After the second tub of water (the first one was absolutely black), he called me in and asked me to burn his shirt and undershirt. I started to protest unthinking, that I could wash them, and he nearly shouted, "Burn them, they smell of death."
>
> Then he asked me to wash his hair which smelled the same, and he was too weak to do it, as he sat in the tub. I soaped and lathered his head twice, but to him the smell still persisted. Eventually, we burned all the clothes he had worn, including his hat, but he could still smell the odor. I thought this was imagination until I got a whiff of the leather watchband he had worn when he sat with his arm around Joe Sylva [*sic:* Sylvia] trying to keep him warm; it had a terrific odor, so we burned that, too.[26]

. . .

Sometimes fire smells of yellowed newspaper clippings; other times it smells of death. Our world can be frightening, full of disease, foolishness, vanity, and apparent waste, but also full of life, art, intelligence, purpose, and frugality—like a rotting or burning log whose nutrients are not lost forever but (evading the chipper or green chain) burrow into the ground to one day rise again in Indian paintbrush, snowberry, and ponderosa pine. Sometimes the losses to fire are incommensurable and the risks disproportionate to the benefits. A good deal of this can only be understood after the fact, and the story binding it all together is often tragic. Worthy of mourning. Not without meaning. The second cairn of loss.

Two facts concerning the fighting of prairie fires that all the XIT hands seem to agree on are that everyone pitched in to put out a fire, whether it was on his property or not, and that fighting was hard work and made a hand hungrier than almost any other activity.
—Cordia Sloan Duke and Joe B. Frantz, *6,000 Miles of Fence*

Fire can and does destroy the resources of the Public Domain. The Bureau of Land Management must be constantly on the alert for this destructive agent. Range and forest fire suppression on lands under the jurisdiction of this office will be given priority over all other Bureau activities, except the safeguarding of human life.
—*1961 Fire Plan for the Prineville Grazing District*

Whereas loss of fire and loss of life are objectively present in smoke-free horizons and granite crosses on windblown ridges, other losses are more "perspectival." They are losses every bit as much as those smoldering in the first two cairns, but they are losses that depend on one's perspective, what one values— whether resources for one's livelihood, a piece of the land that shapes one's identity, or both. For some, these values may be in the shape of a yellow-bellied ponderosa; for others, in crunchy-blond rangeland at the head of a box canyon. Nature is often indifferent to human survival. Likewise, those who applaud "nature's way" are sometimes indifferent to those parts of nature that humans have come to depend on for their livelihoods. Questioning my own indifference began at the margin of a going fire.

Barely a week had passed since the Smith Canyon fire was controlled. And while the pain of Storm King Mountain still clouded the West, more thunderstorms boiled out of the south, scouring the Deschutes and John Day drainages with lightning and feathery virga, those wisps of rain that evaporate before hitting the ground. The North Sherman Fire Department, in Wasco, requested mutual aid for a fast-moving fire burning near the mouth of the John Day River, just south of where it dumps into the Columbia. By midafternoon I was sitting in the cab of Sam Miller's pickup looking down on a terrestrial contrail of fire that stretched all the way from the rim of the canyon to the river five hundred feet below. Sam poured a scalding-hot cup of coffee for himself, and we talked strategy: direct or indirect (that is, up close with a wet gunnysack or shovel, or at a distance setting a backfire), how to deploy the few people we had on hand, and whether air support (like helicopters or retardant planes) was available.

In farming and ranching communities across the West, fires like this one are as much social events as impending disasters. In a world where we increasingly hire professionals to do the jobs we're either too lazy to do or don't know how to do, it's refreshing to see people fend for themselves. At times this devolves into chaos on the fireline, as communication breaks down and eight ranchers and a bartender become the Delta Force of Sherman County. Yet, up to a point, it's hard to cast blame, even if luck has more to do with the outcome than anything. Typically, though, where urban areas sprawl like metastasized cancers into surrounding wildlands, people have neither the skill nor the inclination to fight fire in their own backyards, which—as I'm sure Kierkegaard would agree—is probably for the best. But in many rural communities to this day, when a fire breaks out, so too do the weedsprayers, shovels, and wet gunnysacks. And it doesn't matter when or where the fire is burning.

While my experience fighting fire in Sherman County was primarily one of male dominance at the margins of flames, wives and girlfriends would often drive out to the line delivering cardboard boxes of homemade sandwiches and milk jugs full of iced tea. It used to be that a prerequisite to fighting fire in these parts was a cooler of beer in the truck bed. Now, after years of haranguing by the feds and rural fire districts, most—though not all—coolers just hold pop or water. It doesn't matter who you are or what agency you're with, when the women arrive with sandwiches (sliced diagonally and neatly wrapped in waxed paper), they stop and ask if you're hungry. On a ninety-degree day, the last thing I want is a wad of white bread, mayo, and ham rolling around in my stomach. Yet I always accept the sandwiches. Only a month and a half into the fire season and already having gained the dubious reputation among some Sherman County farmers as the bald-headed son of a bitch, I want to avoid at all cost insulting the farmers' wives.

Occasionally I did run into women who fought fire—like Mary Mauer. Mrs. Mauer looked too old to be fighting fire. But just like clockwork, every time we responded to a fire on her spread above the John Day River near Clarno, she'd already be on the scene with her little metal pail sloshing water and one or two musty gunnies. A modern-day Laura Ingalls Wilder. Ever so slowly, she'd flop her sack at the jagged edge of flame between clumps of sage. All the while she made her husband sit in the pickup, where he wouldn't get in the way or overexert his heart (no doubt get in *her* way and overexert *her* patience).

The fire Sam and I looked down on was near a stretch of rapids called the Narrows, so we called it the Narrows fire. That wouldn't always have been the case; there was a time when we named fires anything we liked. Like the year those of us on the crew decided to adopt a porcine naming protocol. That year, incident reports were adorned with fire names such as Ham, Little Smoky, Bacon, Hog Wild, and many other subtle pig references that I've long since forgotten. Taken individually, our dispatchers and fire managers didn't think twice about the farmyard monikers. Collectively, though, the year-end summary of district fires told a different story. The following summer we were instructed to name fires only after geographic locations.

As at Smith Canyon, this fire had the potential to get big in short order, and also as at Smith Canyon, I was determined not to fry my crew's hide over decadent old sagebrush and cheatgrass butting up against powdery fallow that can't burn (although we sometimes dropped retardant on it anyway). Unlike Smith Canyon, by nightfall we'd have the Narrows fire contained thanks to existing roads and a Sherman County grader.

Every firefighter, no matter how environmentally conscious, reaches a point where getting the job done safely (sometimes just getting the job done) overrides the dictum of "light hand on the land." (Maybe everyone does this at some point no matter what the project or task in life. Even a perfectionist will, on the verge of frustration and up against deadlines, say, "To hell with it; that's good enough.") Light-hand tactics attempt to control fire through the least environmentally invasive means possible: instead of dozerline, you construct handline (with a shovel or pulaski); instead of handline, you hose down vegetation, forming a wetline, or smother fire with a gunny sack; instead of constructing any line, you use natural barriers to stop the fire. But with multiple fires burning, few people to fight them, and more hot and dry weather forecasted, my days as a light-hand purist were in the past. I suggested to Sam that we take the county grader and carve a control line down a side ridge to the river. From that fuel-free scrape we'd backfire.

Sam agreed. First, though, he and a few others wanted to have a go at Old Man Devil hand-to-hand style—Sherman County style. Within half an hour Sam was clawing his way out of the canyon, face beet red and his yellow fireshirt soaked with sweat.

"It spanked us good," Sam said, still out of breath.

Abandoning the direct method, we backed off to the ridge, dropped the blade beneath the grader, and scraped a line to mineral soil from the fallow fields above to the John Day's murky waters below. I'm sure that by now the only evidence that fire ever burned above the Narrows is a twelve-foot-wide strip of cheatgrasss that connects the rim with the river. It pains me to think of our damage to the landscape, but much of the fire was on private land where a twelve-foot-wide scar filled with cheat is still more acceptable than one season of black. This may seem shortsighted, and maybe it is. It's especially shortsighted in the eyes of suburbanites who pay someone else to fight their fires.

The grader was almost to the river when we started backfiring. Sam did most of the lighting, with my engine easing down the ridge behind him to hose down spotfires that had crossed the line or to cool flaming brush on the fire side of the line that might spark a spotfire. I'll never forget the image of Sam—blue bandana wrapped over his balding head, black rubber piss bag (a.k.a. backpack pump) on his back, cigarette dangling out of his mouth—stooped over lighting the grass with a fusee (the firefighter's equivalent of a road flare).

Evening came and we congratulated ourselves over our good fortune: not too many tempers had flared, the fire was contained, and nobody was injured. We wouldn't get much sleep that night, however. About 11 PM we received a report of another fire burning along the John Day River east of Grass Valley, about twenty miles to our south. Job security.

In the glow of his cab's domelight, Sam looked over at me, grinned, and in a low, gravelly voice said: "Well, little man, let's go fight some fire."

...

The summer of 1994 proved that when it comes to firefighting, rote memorization of procedures, strategy, and tactics is not good enough. More often than not, you must improvise. Sometimes the key is major; sometimes it is minor. Rarely will you know the chord progression in advance.

Throughout the next morning and afternoon we rehearsed the same old licks that we had tried at Smith Canyon and the Narrows: descend into the canyon with a tool and wet gunnysack and try to stop the fire directly. The fire burned in Little Ferry Canyon, a large, brush-choked drainage on the west side of the John Day River. Again, since both BLM and private lands checkerboarded the canyon, Sam and I jointly supervised the firefighting effort.

As the morning inversion lifted and the already-dehydrated vegetation began to bake, it was apparent that we had more fire—more stubborn fire that kept restarting—than our skimpy crews could handle. So we put the same county road grader that had been on the Narrows fire to work blading a line around Little Ferry then back to the rim of the John Day River. There we hoped to pinch the fire off in a slide of Columbia River basalt. One problem, though, was that the grader line came perilously close to the boundary of a BLM Wilderness Study Area (WSA). In theory, WSAs must be treated like wilderness until the U.S. Congress makes up its mind whether or not to officially designate them wilderness. Much to the chagrin of our BLM resource adviser, the grader had weaved in and out of the WSA. For years to come, Little Ferry would no doubt be rimmed by twelve-foot-wide strips of opportunistic cheatgrass that had invaded the ripped-up soil. But the damage was done, and we had a clean fuel-break from which to backfire. The final one-eighth mile of line above the rockslide was simply a two-track jeep trail, clearly within the WSA boundary. With fire engine support, we planned to burn from the bare tracks.

That would change when our helicopter radioed with the news that the fire had slipped around the rockslide and into the next drainage to the north—Deep Canyon. Sam and I decided to extend the grader line north, between standing winter wheat, CRP grass, and the headend of Deep Canyon. There we would tie in with another two-track road. We would backfire along the two-track for a mile to the north, where the road connected with the blackened remnants of an early-season fire that had already burned from the river to the canyon rim. At the end of the day, Little Ferry Canyon and Deep Canyon would be smoking black pits, the fire contained.

Sam rounded up a group of ranchers and a county fire engine, then headed to the old burn. From there they'd lay fire toward the south. I'd work the BLM helitack crew and another handful of ranchers to fire from Little Ferry to the north. Somewhere in the middle we'd drive a flaming spike of fire in the brush, and the backfire would be complete. But it was time for yet another key shift when the pilot notified me that a man on a bulldozer was trying to hook the northeast corner of fire—the flank that had already slopped around the rock scree to the north and was clawing its way up Deep Canyon. I had visions of Smith all over again: a backfire put on hold for some damned impatient freelancer(s). This time, however, there would be no heroic conclusion. It was too late for heroism, and I was determined to get him out of there so we could light our torches and get on with business.

Anyone who thinks that all there is to fighting fire is simply squirting water, throwing dirt, or creating a fuel-break is sadly mistaken. On hot summer evenings atop the Columbia Plateau, when the fires of summer wend their way from the public domain onto private land and then back onto public once again, to engage fire means to talk: about crops, about weather, about bunchgrass and wheatgrass and decadent old sage and cheat that would be no worse for the wear if it flamed out under the fading light of a July sun. So I drove to the end of the ridge to find the dozer operator . . . and talk.

I cringed when I realized that the jeep trail shown on my map was now a naked dozerline bounded by two berms of powdery tan soil and loose tufts of grass. Near the end of the ridge I caught sight of the dozer—a D8 Cat—just below the crest of the ridgeline and carving a trail through the brush in advance of flames that were now backing up the slope. Several half circles of soot-stained dirt fanned out in the smoldering grass to his east—

earlier attempts to block what was only the tip of a "fireberg" surfacing in the canyon below. "What the hell is he thinking?" I thought.

I'm sure that the man on the dozer thought, "Who the hell is he?" as I waved at him to hold up. Finally he pulled out of the advancing flames, into the black, and slipped the transmission of the peeling yellow hulk into neutral. I climbed onto the tracks, introduced myself (though I can't remember if he gave me his name), and told him that the fire was already in Deep Canyon and that we intended to burn out the area where we now stood. Even an emotionless look can show disgust. The man was probably in his sixties. The wrinkles on his deep-furrowed face were filled in with dust and ash, and his bib overalls were stained with what was no doubt hydraulic fluid from the cracked, leaking hoses of the dozer. His hat read "Sherman Co-Op."

He began by telling me that the fire was burning on his land. He then went on at length to inform me that the helicopter *could* have stopped the fire if the damn thing hadn't flown off. If even one person would have been down over the ridge, he could have put out the fire by just scuffing the ground with his boots. Someone could have caught the fire, if only . . .

I felt the man was wrong on both counts. The land wasn't his. My map showed Deep Canyon as mainly BLM, with only a few scattered forty-acre parcels of private. The "freeway" that he bladed along the ridgeline separating Deep Canyon to the north from Little Ferry Canyon to the south was definitely in a WSA (though the road we planned to burn from was private). Second, his brand of hindsight was commonplace in my experience of working with private landowners. I've heard countless stories on countless other fires where if so-and-so had just gotten one more helicopter bucket drop, or one more person with a shovel, or one more fire engine—one more something—he or she could have stopped the fire. Maybe so. Most likely not. What the man driving the Cat didn't see was what the pilot saw—a string of fire that had swung around the ridge and was headed up Deep Canyon; what he didn't hear was the radio traffic that crews were having trouble back in Little Ferry Canyon and needed helicopter bucket drops; what he didn't know was that there were other fires burning across the Pacific Northwest and that only a few BLM firefighters were available to help on this incident.

I'd never met the man before. He probably wished he'd never met me. But there we were: me crouching on the idled tracks practically yelling over the engine noise, the landowner sitting, shaking his head and repeating that we *could* have caught the fire "if only." Finally, I agreed.

"Maybe so," I said. But I explained that since the fire was too dangerous to fight directly in Deep Canyon, our only good option was to back off to the road and backfire to the north, to the margin of the old burn. If we didn't do this the fire would no doubt roar out of the ravine like a stoked furnace, jump the anemic two-track, then spread into CRP grass and cured winter wheat and possibly even the backyards of Grass Valley. If not today, definitely tomorrow. But it would be his call, since we'd be burning from his road.

[91]

Still shaking his head, he said in a barely audible voice, "That's my winter feed down there."

I couldn't help but think, *You've got to be kidding—crunchy yellow cheatgrass and sage—damn fine winter range, indeed.* I shrugged my shoulders and reciprocated the negative head shake, trying to communicate, "So . . . what now?"

We both looked down on the fire that was making an end run around his meandering dozerline. Fire was well into Deep Canyon, smoke bending updrainage, rising to the elevation of the rim, then catching a stiff northwest breeze and rolling back on top of itself, like ocean breakers.

With a sigh, he finally said, "Okay."

I told him that as soon as he walked the Cat back to the road, we'd begin lighting.

...

In *A Sand County Almanac,* Aldo Leopold laments the disappearance of the wolf from the desert Southwest, even noting his own role in snuffing out the "fierce green fire" in the eyes of these creatures. He writes that "the cowman who cleans his range of wolves does not realize that he is taking over the wolf's job of trimming the herd to fit the range. He has not learned to think like a mountain. Hence we have dustbowls and rivers washing the future into the sea."[1] The cowman and deer hunter saw wolves as mere impediments to what they viewed as the truly valuable resources offered up by the land—beef and venison. From the human perspective, the losses resulting from wolves might seem unacceptable. But from the perspective of, say, a

[92]

mountain (metaphorically speaking), seemingly unredeemable losses take on the shade of ecological good. "Only the mountain has lived long enough to listen objectively to the howl of a wolf."[2] In fact, Leopold's point was that wolves regulate deer such that severe overgrazing by exploding deer populations rarely occurs. When wolves are removed for the sake of beef and venison, a chain of events unfurls, leading from more deer to less grass to fewer deer and finally, fewer cows. In the end you have hardpan and brush, little venison or beef, "and rivers washing the future into the sea."

Perspective. In mountain time—ecological time—death often promotes life.[3] Green Gambel oak sprouting from the bases of black sticks confirms the resilience of earth and life. Sometimes the keystone species is the wolf or bear or lynx. Other times it's wind, rain, or fire.

Today there are no wolves lurking in the margins of standing wheat and summer fallow in Sherman County. For many, fire is carnivore enough.[4] I don't think it's too far afield to extend Leopold's metaphor to fire: the rancher who cleans his range of fire doesn't realize that he is taking over fire's job of trimming the range. Once fire-sensitive sagebrush is leveled to smoking black stobs, fire-tolerant bunchgrass survives in its root crown, beneath delicate, incinerated stems. Bunches of Idaho fescue and bluebunch wheatgrass may even grow back more luxuriant than before the fire. The canyon knows this, but the rancher often does not. This is the mystery. Sitting atop his D8, the rancher was the perfect metaphor—even caricature—of agriculture and

[93]

culture in the West: one man heroically battling nature for the sake of resources that he wants from nature, blind to how those resources came upon the landscape in the first place, as if each year's crop of grass or each growth ring of a tree had sprung spontaneously into existence without the help of nutrients in the soil or elements in the air.

For me, it was a clear-cut decision of costs and benefits to torch Deep Canyon. It was safer to backfire from the top of the canyon with the wind in our favor than descend into the canyon, where we'd be chasing fire for days, only to wind up on top the ridge in the end. More important, there would be little if anything lost by touching off the canyon: old sequoia-size sagebrush long overdue to burn, bunchgrass that would be invigorated by the burning, and cheatgrass that could be either helped or hindered, though hopefully hindered. Burn it and let the range live, I thought. If we caught a few of the rufous-sided, shit-splattered hayburners (otherwise known as Herefords) in the barbecue, that's the cost of doing business in a land that burns. By next spring Little Ferry Canyon and Deep Canyon would be draped in emerald. I'd seen it before, where a rancher laments the loss of his rangeland only to eat crow by next season when a grass crop returns that he hasn't seen in, well, as long as he can remember.

However, mountain time—canyon time—isn't always amenable to human time. In these cases it isn't clear whose timepiece to use. Knowing that it was probably the catskinner's wife who doled out individually wrapped sandwiches earlier in the day, and that I sat on the tracks of an idling Cat controlled by a hopping-mad farmer whose land I was about to burn, I refrained from playing the ecological optimist. Mountain-time judgments are much easier from the cool repose of distance and winter; quoting Leopold along the dusty rim of the John Day River—even if philosophically and ecologically evocative—would have revealed me for the federal bastard that the catskinner probably suspected me of being.

There's little reason to expect a canyonside epiphany from a man on a bulldozer. Not immediately, at least. Some of the land that the man claimed as his own in Deep Canyon was colored bright yellow on my map—BLM land, public land. In a way, though, it was his, and more literally than some generalized notion of "public" ownership: he owned the grazing rights. And in a system of range management historically synchronized with human time, ecological degradation was not totally his fault. Where at least three generations of Sherman County ranchers have seen land in various stages of decline, what may be historically anomalous to the mountain has moved into the category of humanly normal: "That's the way it's always looked." "That's my winter pasture." Beef is the crop, fed by what grass there is, and any reduction of grass smacks of less beef on the scales. Fire burns feed, therefore fire must be stopped. But what if it isn't? Why not think like a mountain, a canyon, a landscape? In the end there still might be room for cows, deer, wolves, and fire. That is, if you're still in business.

Here's the rub. Even if the rancher knows that fire can bring benefits, even if he knows that a fresh crop of grass will resprout

[95]

out of scorched earth (and that withholding fire might even work against the very things he values), winter is just a few months away and cows need to eat. Unlike wheat farmers I've met in some parts of the country who seem to be living quite lavishly off section upon section of grain en route to overseas ports, most of the farmer-ranchers I know in Sherman County are just getting by, and not much more. Rank feed is still feed, no matter how you look at it; and blackened tufts that disintegrate like lantern mantles are not feed, though they will be in a season or two. In the meantime there are bills to pay and cattle to feed and hay to purchase to feed the cattle. Loss—genuine, real, possibly permanent.

The same could be said of other livelihoods dependent on resources susceptible to fire, from small woodlots to forests to fields of crops. When they go up in smoke, it may or may not be an ecological disaster. More often than not it isn't. As Nancy Langston has said, "What would be threatened by insect epidemics and catastrophic fires is not the forest, but our ability to extract certain resources." Regardless of the fire's intensity—sterilizing some soils and skimming lightly over others, thinning some stands of timber and leveling others to ashen moonscapes—a new path of succession and life will unfold, and to the mountain and canyon, a path not necessarily for the worse. But where culture has silted over Sherman County's native ecology with wheat and barley or cows, we enter a different time zone: until combines reduce fields to stubble or alternate range is found for winter, fire is never welcome; mountain time isn't even considered.[5]

Protecting areas from fire for economic reasons is nothing new. Even though American Indians had nothing approaching either the infrastructure or the inclination to suppress fire on the scale that we have for the last century, there is evidence that they occasionally protected areas from fire because of the plants grown there or the role those spots served as wildlife habitat.[6] Although fire most certainly stimulates the growth of many subsistence crops (and the loss of this fire—the first cairn—consequently leads to the loss of livelihood), if it chews through an area at the wrong time of year, it can ruin that year's harvest. Hence, through either actively swatting out flames or firing around areas to be protected (even if that amounted merely to taking defensive measures to protect their campsites or villages), Indians, too, excluded fire for economic reasons.[7]

These were all nonissues as I crawled off the dozer tracks and rejoined my crew to begin backfiring. Mountain time and fading hours of daylight saving time were my main concerns.

. . .

With the D8 and its operator out of the way, we commenced firing. A stiff northwest wind sailed over the rim, pulling our backfire away from the dusty two-track into a unity of flame that bled into Deep Canyon to connect with the convecting upgulch hemorrhage. My squad of lighters, armed with watering can–like driptorches that dribbled strips of incandescent diesel and gasoline, practically ran to finish burning before the wind shifted or the fire in the canyon gained momentum and spilled to the top of the draw.

Behind the lighters crept a string of vehicles meant to hold the backfire in check. First came a BLM fire engine, then a half dozen Road Warrioresque farm and ranch trucks. Every dust-caked rig was customized for the day-to-day rituals of harvest and fence building or to engage the fires of summer when they inevitably groped their way out of Sherman County canyons into standing wheat. Though different, each was a variation on a similar theme: rats' nests of barbed wire and orange plastic baling twine coiled around rusted tools, empty beer cans, and pump plumbing; a cow dog pirouetting around the cluttered truck bed and onto the toolbox or bale of hay to get a better view; the wife and kids filling the bench seat in the dusty cab. Some farmhand, son or daughter, walks behind the creeping truck dragging a weedsprayer hose, squirting down flaming fence posts. When not used for fire, their water tanks brim over with herbicides for the ongoing battle against weeds. I couldn't help but wonder how a mild solution of herbicides reacts to fire.

Rounding the dogleg in the road, I caught sight of Sam's group approaching from the north. No lighters jogged in front of their caravan; instead, a propane torch protruded from the driver's-side window of the lead pickup. Creative. When the two groups met, the lead vehicles sat nose to nose where, for a moment, everyone seemed to be asking, "What next?" It was a rare coordinated effort in the confrontation of fire on the border of public and private domain. The answer to "What next?" came as the propane torch swallowed up its flame, my lighters blew out their driptorch wicks, and a great sea of fire piled up to our east as the sun set over the Cascades to the west. Deep Canyon was gutted.

A little later, after most of the ranchers either returned home or dispersed to other parts of the fire, a helitack crewman named George and I drove to where we could get a good view of our handiwork. I remember walking out between sparking sage and rabbit brush to where I could look into Deep Canyon, now awash in a constellation of flickering orange, red, and yellow. It would have made a great photograph. Fire can be beautiful, particularly at night—not just because of the brilliant colors, but because of the amazing translation of matter into energy taking place before one's eyes.

Norman Maclean suggested that the firefighters who died in Mann Gulch passed an aesthetic "station of the cross": a point where the expanding blowup was arrestingly beautiful, even to those in its path. One firefighter was seen snapping pictures of the very same flame front that moments later overtook him, searing his lungs and charring his body. This would be their last aesthetic moment on their way to their last breaths along their last fire.[8] Fire can be sublime, stopping one along an escape route just long enough to see what no one else has, or ever will, see again. That life and things of value are lost in the flames does not necessarily negate the aesthetic qualities of fire, nor does short-term destruction and seeming chaos necessarily blot out the ecological beauty of life moving from form to formlessness, which in time nurtures new form. Mountain time. However, the optimism of mountain time does not obviate the genuine losses of the present: ecological beauty does not take away the fact that thirteen men died in Mann Gulch, or that a Sherman County farmer may face bankruptcy because his cows can't eat ashes.

But all I thought about as I looked into Deep Canyon was the rare privilege to gaze upon nature combusting: the sight of sparks dissolving into the Big Dipper accompanied by the sound of snapping wood and the clank of rolling rocks, dislodged as their moss-encasing nests disintegrated into ash.

In tribute to all Sam Miller had taught me about the Sherman County vernacular of fire, I cocked my head back, cleared my throat, and hawked a chunk of phlegm over the rim.

"Take that, Old Man Devil," I said.

...

Deep Canyon was nearly smoke-free by first light. Range fires have a habit of doing this—quickly skimming over lichen-encrusted soils or melting slender grass stalks into a thin bed of coals. Fall rains and winter snows eventually swept across north central Oregon. By late spring, new growth carpeted the slopes of Little Ferry Canyon and Deep Canyon. From the air, with the exception of a few scorched juniper trees and a twelve-foot-wide ribbon of cheatgrass just starting to turn purple, it was nearly impossible to tell that ten months earlier a small part of the world had become fire.

Before the start of the 1995 fire season I attended a public meeting in the Sherman County High School cafeteria. Several gray-haired women prepared big metal trays of lasagna and buttered loaves of French bread that we all grazed on before the formal presentations began. The goal of the meeting was to plan how to cooperate on future fires in Sherman County. The county judge opened by congratulating everyone for taking the time to show up, with special thanks to the women who had prepared supper. The BLM district manager and fire management officer gave speeches explaining federal fire-suppression policy. I gave a short talk outlining the "Ten Standard Fire Orders" and the "Eighteen Situations That Shout Watch Out."

After the meeting, the Cat driver who I'd negotiated with on the ridge between Little Ferry and Deep Canyons the summer before introduced himself to me. I hardly recognized him. The heavy-set man wore a pair of clean, bright blue overalls and no hat. We shook hands. He mentioned how tempers can flare along a fireline. I agreed. I wanted to ask how his cows fared over the winter, but I didn't. Did he have to sell off his herd? Did he have other winter pastures? Was it a financially lean winter? His presence in the school cafeteria suggested that, regardless of his cows, he had retained his roots in Sherman County. I'm not entirely sure what to make of that. Sometimes there's a fine line between mountain time and human time, and like tragedy, that line is often discernible only after the fact. Some things that we depend on for our livelihoods are worth saving, even if in theory we might have lived a different way and even if those things we've come to depend on naturally burn.

The only conclusion I have ever reached about trees is that I love all trees, but I am in love with pines.
—Aldo Leopold, *A Sand County Almanac*

He died protecting his pines. It was spring 1948, and Aldo Leopold was spending time with his family at their beloved cabin they called "the Shack." Over the years, he had planted close to thirty thousand trees and shrubs on the property, trying to resuscitate a tired Wisconsin sand farm into some semblance of ecological health. Leopold was keenly aware of fire's natural role in ecosystems, but sometimes there's more to fire and living with fire than energy flow, nutrient flush, and plant physiology.[1]

During the Leopolds' stay at the Shack, a neighbor's trash fire, fanned by a west wind, escaped its bounds and threatened to overtake the pines. Alone along one flank of the fire, Aldo suffered a heart attack and was later found dead, lying on his back in the smoldering grass.[2] For the love of pines.

In *A Sand County Almanac*, accepted for publication just one week before his death, Leopold explores several possible reasons for his bias toward pines: maybe it's because he planted the pines, or pines are rare where he lives, or pines have a longer life expectancy than other trees, or pines are evergreens, or because his neighbors don't have many pines on their land, or pines are worth more to the lumberman than other species, or pines engender more plant diversity than other species. In the end, he concludes that "our plant biases reflect not only vocations but avocations, with a delicate allocation of priority as between industry and indolence. The farmer who would rather hunt grouse than milk cows will not dislike hawthorn, no matter if it does invade his pasture. The coon-hunter will not dislike basswood, and I know of quail hunters who bear no grudge against ragweed, despite their annual bout with hay fever. Our biases are indeed a sensitive index to our affections, our tastes, our loyalties, our generosities, and our manner of wasting weekends."[3]

Leopold's last act in life—fighting a fire endangering something he valued—testifies to the tension between mountain time and human time. It's doubtful that the landscape around the Shack would have suffered permanent damage even if the fire overran his pines. Some trees would have burned and died, but eventually the land would revegetate and more pines could be planted. But as humans who, according to the psalmist, live but "threescore and ten, or even by reason of strength fourscore,"[4] we may never see our pines or any other part of the landscape fully healed, assuming it even can be. One tree, or grove of trees, is not necessarily interchangeable with another. Places can be lost and never replaced. This is one reason why the philosopher Robert Elliot is so skeptical of ecological restoration. Like a work of art, simply replacing it, even with the most exacting replica, will never fully replace the original, for part of an object's value derives from its history: who painted or sculpted it, when it was crafted, the reason behind its contours and colors.[5] Not only are exact replicas in nature hard to come by (even though our science and technology of restoration is improving), but some values can never be restored.

Some things are worth protecting from fire simply because they're important to us—even a part of us—and not necessarily because they're resources on their way to becoming beef, venison, or two-by-fours. What's critical, though, as we struggle to live in a land that burns, is getting clear how we want that land to look and why. I fear that we've become so transfixed by the power of ecological-sounding arguments—scientific-sounding arguments gilded with graphs and statistics—that either we fail to recognize how values permeate our ecology or we downplay the legitimacy of preserving parts of nature for other than strictly ecological or economic reasons.

Those of us who advocate restoring fire to western ecosystems as often as not pawn off aesthetic, philosophical, or economic reasons for ecological reasons. Take so-called "open, parklike" stands of ponderosa pine as the crème de la crème of restoration by fire. Invariably, if you wander into some academic or professional lecture on fire and ecological restoration, you'll be treated to the obligatory slide show of "repeat photography" (that is, photographs taken at the turn of the twentieth century—representing presettlement landscapes—compared with photos of the same site today). True, lack of fire has greatly altered the look of the land; however, part of what led to today's look is not a lack of lightning or our sophisticated firefighting technology, but the smothering of indigenous peoples and their fires. As a result, some of the early photos in repeat photography sequences do not merely depict "natural" conditions but show landscapes influenced by cultural uses of fire.[6] The fires that American Indians mingled with the land were primarily economic—intentionally set to nurture plants for food, basketry, or forage (though, of course, these fires had ecological effects). America's first peoples didn't pass between the ice into a land begging for restoration; rather, they entered a continent in ecological flux as climate changed, a land that for thousands of years thence they would shape by fire to supply their needs.

I once read a newspaper article in which presettlement forests were described as "beautiful" and "durable."[7] In discussions regarding ecological restoration, you'll often hear stock phrases such as "open, parklike stands," and "frequent, low-intensity fires." I'm sure that many presettlement forests were beautiful, often parklike, and often swept by low-intensity fires, especially in the drier, low-elevation forests of the Intermountain West. But confusing nature with what we want from nature does little to help us reinhabit the West in the present. Are we really interested in harvesting camas roots and berries or grazing large bands of horses? If not, what are we trying to recreate if many of the parklike stands in the nineteenth-century photos were artifacts of root, berry, and horse economies? For instance, Nancy Langston points out that "if we assume that presettlement fire regimes were natural and therefore necessary, the logic falls apart if it turns out that those fires were of very recent origin, say only after the 1730s, when Indians acquired horses and wanted open forest stands to encourage forage for the horses and to make horseback hunting easier."[8] Or do we just like open parks? At some deep, subconscious level, do they remind us of the African savannas into which our ancient ancestors entered after descending from trees, straightening their backs, and walking upright?[9]

If we want to bolster deer and elk populations, reduce fire risk, increase populations of species dependent on old-growth ponderosa pine (old growth that in many cases only existed because of indigenous fire practices), then we're embracing predominately cultural, not ecological, reasons for our land management. If we can't afford either to let fires run their course (because of what fire might consume) or to suppress unwelcome fires once they get going (to keep budgets balanced), then maybe prescribed fire is a prudent, cost-effective solution—a primarily *nonecologically* motivated solution.

The point where mountain time ends and human time begins is often shrouded in the haze of human-crafted landscapes. Yet even when the inversion breaks and our cultural reasons—be they love of sparse forests or love of pines—become apparent, we need to resolve whether these values are sometimes worth preserving in their own right. I believe they are; our identities may depend on it. And maybe preserving some things because we love them is part of *our* ecology.

• • •

In the world that the Western Apaches have constituted for themselves, features of the landscape have become symbols of and for this way of living, the symbols of a culture and the enduring moral character of its people.[10]

In his excellent book, *Wisdom Sits in Places*, the ethnologist Keith Basso describes how Western Apache place names signify more than mere points on a map—they tell stories. Simply mentioning the names of places, like "Shades of Shit" or "Trail Goes Down Between Two Hills," conjures up images of not only physical geography but also events for which the places are named and the meanings wrapped up in those events. Uttering a place name in the right context is all that is needed to communicate a message of reproach, admonishment, or encouragement—that is, a way of conveying the moral geography of a place.

Frequently, though, we are inattentive to places until their very existence is in jeopardy. "It is then," writes Basso, that "we come to see that attachments to places may be nothing less than profound, and that when these attachments are threatened we may feel threatened as well. Places, we realize, are as much a part of us as we are part of them, and senses of place—yours, mine, and everyone else's—partake complexly of both."[11]

While I want to believe that wild places, places that are only minimally altered by human influence, are vitally important to understanding who we are and ought to become, meaning-laden places needn't be purely natural or wild.[12] A building, a particular spot in a brick plaza, a street, or a monument all carry meanings and tell stories—stories of others and stories of ourselves.

To the extent that these places (be they rocks, trees, or park benches) become physical and moral fixtures in our world—our habitat—they remind us of who we are and who we should be. If a place is altered or destroyed, everything that it symbolized starts to blur. Depending on how much of our own personal history is bound up in that site, when its meanings start to blur, we too may feel dislocated.

Few of us would be so crass as to say our homes mean nothing to us. The houses in which we live and the belongings we accumulate are part of our habitat. Sometimes our habitat may become so choked with detritus that a good hot fire might actually do us some good. Still, the things we surround ourselves with can take on deep significance, linking us to our past and reminding us of who we are. Is there any reason that our concept of home can't extend beyond the confines of brick and Sheetrock and glass to fixed points in nature?

When I ask myself "Who am I?" I don't imagine pure Mind—disembodied spark of the divine, intelligible apart from time and experience. "Experience" in my case is hopelessly (and hopefully) rooted in places. I think of growing up in a rental house on a farm in the northern Willamette Valley; I think of blackberry thickets and brushrows that were my forts and my nature preserves; I think about trout streams and college campuses, rimrock and creeping fires in the northern Great Basin. In my waking hours I move through places, reminisce about places, and look forward to places—some artifactual, some natural, some a mix of both; my dreams choreograph life amidst places, some real, some imagined, all physical. To forget the geography of my past is to forget who I am. According to Basso, "Long before the advent of literacy, to say nothing of 'history' as an academic discipline, places served humankind as durable symbols of distant events and as indispensable aids for remembering and imagining them."[13]

So places not only anchor us in space and time, they symbolically tie us to our past. Regarding wilderness, the farmer and nature writer Wendell Berry writes that "these places function . . . whether we intend them to or not, as sacred groves—places we respect and leave alone, not because we understand well what goes on there, but because we do not."[14] Sacred groves—understood as places where ancient processes of nature are allowed to run their course, more or less without human interference—reside in mountain time.

But other sacred groves are sacred because they are groves, because the ancient organisms in their midst carry meaning beyond potential fuel for fire. Our sacred groves can range from personal, unknown to anyone beyond ourselves, to communal to national. It might be a solitary tree, a meadow, grove, or forest. It might be the largest tree in Montana (like the ponderosa pine that clings to the banks of Fish Creek in the Bitterroots), a grove of ancient redwoods, or the soft white bark of an aspen into which two lovers inscribed their initials. There will always be some degree of flux and fluidity and change to places (from trees layering on growth rings or outcompeting their neighbors for sunlight, to streets and buildings and statues weathering with time). As the poet and naturalist Gary Snyder says, "A place will have been grasslands, then conifers, then beech and elm. It will have been half riverbed, it will have been scratched and plowed by ice. And then it will be cultivated, paved, sprayed, dammed, graded, built up. But each is only for a while, and that will just be another set of lines on the palimpsest. The whole earth is a great tablet holding the multiple overlaid new and ancient traces of the swirl of forces."[15]

However, not every swirl (be it water or fire) can or should be lovingly embraced, for our own mortality bears down with the message: threescore and ten . . . and if you're lucky, fourscore. I don't want that aspen cut or burned, not in my lifetime. Is that selfish, ecologically myopic? Maybe, though not necessarily. Is it just another example of human domination, control, an intellectual hand-me-down of Francis Bacon? Again, maybe, though not necessarily. That big old pine up Fish Creek might provide damned good trout habitat for westslope cutthroat if it topples into the stream after its roots burn out; but every once in a while, I like to see big old things. Maybe we love pines that we planted. Maybe we just love pines.

. . .

For a number of years I hunted elk along the southeast corner of Oregon's Malheur National Forest. From where I camped, the country sloughed off to the south toward the dormant caldera of Malheur Lake, now a national wildlife refuge. To the east, little tributaries sliced through deposits of petrified wood and agate on their way to the Malheur River. It was "fringe country"—that elevation where thick pine and fir give way to open sagebrush flats and pockets of mountain mahogany and juniper. In the drainages and around seeps that weren't trampled to death by cattle (which weren't that many), aspen clumped up. In the late September sun these bright yellow bouquets announced places to search for elk wallows.

One day while hunting, I found a small stand of ponderosa pine on the edge of a sagebrush scabflat just a quarter mile from camp. Three of the trees were massive, probably at least five feet across at their butts. I was shocked that they hadn't been cut and hauled to the mill in Hines. Their isolation from the more sprawling stands of pine higher up probably made them a headache to extract. Or maybe the timber cruisers and lumber companies were just getting around to ringing them with blue paint and skidding them out to an idling Peterbilt. Either way, they were big and old—no doubt some of the most ancient trees remaining on the entire Malheur.

No "Point of Interest" markers led Bermuda shorts–clad tourists along a pea-gravel path to some damnable interpretive sign. It wasn't a wilderness area, a wilderness study area, or any other designation that would show up on a map and attract gawkers to shit in the pine needles at the trees' bases. They were just three beautiful trees on the north side of a scabby opening above Pine Creek.

I napped under the trees on bright Indian summer days. Little vegetation grew around their trunks. Instead the ground was carpeted with flaked reddish brown bark—like miniature puzzle pieces—overlain with golden needles. One morning, just a few feet from the pines, I hunkered behind a mahogany thicket and bugled in a three-point bull to within five yards of my nocked arrow. I didn't dare move as the elk stared through the green curled leaves, stretched his neck forward, and whistled a raspy squeal. It was too brushy to get a clean shot, and I was too exposed to move without being seen, so I sat motionless and just watched the frustrated bull walk away—neither an antler-tangling fight nor an orgasm to show for himself.

In the evenings as our campfire of juniper and mahogany melted to pumpkin orange coals, my partners and I would share what we saw during the day. Invariably someone would comment on those big pines and how they escaped the Stihls and Husqvarnas. Those pines symbolized endurance and stability. They conjured up memories of fall days, rutting elk, and learning to be satisfied with tawny rumps lumbering away from still-nocked arrows.

Several years ago I learned that a fire had swept through the area of the three big pines. I have yet to return for fear of finding nothing but blackened snags or postsalvage stumps. Maybe, though, the trees weathered the firestorm, as they no doubt have weathered numerous other fires throughout their Adamic lives. Then again, I know that even hardy trees, like ponderosa, can succumb to fire if the weather is hot and dry and windy. Why can't I just accept the potential loss in stride, resting in the afterglow of what once was, drinking in the knowledge that nature is taking its course (that is, like a good, optimistic, ecologically informed and aesthetically sensitive inhabitant of the contemporary American West)? Because it's a place that matters, a place whose history overlaps with my history, with my identity. The headwaters of the Malheur River are probably no worse for the wear if three pillars of charcoal now stand as testaments to the ancient mix of cloud and lightning and dry fuel. If the climate someday again turns cool and moist enough to allow seedlings to establish themselves on what is today a marginal site for pines, centuries hence new hulks will shelter reddish puzzle pieces and yellow needles, and other elk will squeal and mate beneath their formidable shade. On the flip side, if these three trees didn't melt into charcoal and evaporate into smoke, the system of life on the Malheur would also be no worse for the wear. And when it comes to judging whether protecting an area from fire is acceptable or not, maybe it's a matter of scale—human and ecological; loss of place to fire versus ecological loss from the loss of fire.

Protecting places from natural forces can be justified, although, practically speaking, it must be selective. There is no way that government agencies entrusted with smothering fire can know the personal significance that every place in the West has to every living resident of the West. If this were possible, it still wouldn't be desirable to freeze the continent in a scenic and ecological ice age.[16] In fact, preserving components of the landscape that we value—and in which we ground our identity—may be less a matter of excluding all fire than of figuring out a way to invite fire back in, since fire may have been the very force that created the landscape characteristics that we value. Here, the first cairn (loss of fire) informs the fourth (loss of place).

I want to give voice to the power of places, but I know that for many people place attachments are so diffuse as to be trivial: generalized and sentimentalized pretty scenes that say nothing of how they came to be or what they would take to maintain. Hence, we're faced with the dilemma pointed out by the conservationist and wilderness advocate Bob Marshall: "A pessimist would conclude that one summer's fires destroyed more beauty than all the inhabitants of the earth could create in many years, while an optimist would go singing through that blackened, misshapened world rejoicing because the forest will look just as beautiful as before—in two or three centuries. Take your choice."[17] It's always possible that such generalized aesthetics might hold the same identity-forming power that very particular places hold; nevertheless, when amplified beyond the occasional tree or grove to entire watersheds and regions, we've probably moved from the discipline of geriatrics to cryogenics—beyond ecological intubation to landscape embalming.

I inhabit places and they are my habitat: some of which change, some of which I hope won't change anytime soon. Though I'm unsure if we can properly claim to have relationships with places (as we do with persons), surely particular places do ground us physically, emotionally, and spiritually. In philosophical terms, they even inform us "epistemologically," for they help us know where we've come from, which is another way of saying they help us know who we are. Some skeptics may remain unconvinced: Memories are good enough. We're adaptable creatures and can always find new habitats in which to dwell, new symbols in which to invest meaning. But in my estimation, these amount to cold abstractions. I want to feel space, to smell the past, to run my hands over the same pine bark that a bull elk raked his antlers against, the same tree that I napped under years ago. I want to feel the past in the present. When these connections are severed, grief is appropriate.

I can relate to Leopold's decision never to revisit the Delta of Colorado after he and his brother first canoed there in 1922: "It is the part of wisdom never to revisit a wilderness, for the more golden the lily, the more certain that someone has gilded it. To return not only spoils a trip, but tarnishes a memory. It is only in the mind that shining adventure remains forever bright." The memories of places—even just their names—encode whole stories. Consequently, it's important that some places retain the shape in which we remember them: for the sake of revisiting them and for the sake of just knowing that they are there. Though he was writing about wilderness, the words of Wendell Berry also apply to any area that embodies special meaning and value, for "whether we go to those places or not, we need to know that they exist." This is one reason that historical sites like Gettysburg are kept from reentering the stream of ecological succession. There is historical value in maintaining some tracts of land—their trees, their fields, their wildlife—as they were when the events occurred for which they are now remembered.[18]

Again, change is inevitable—mountain time demands it. But some change can be arrested—human time needs it.

No doubt there comes a time when grief is inevitable, for that which we've come to love struggles for air with collapsing lungs and dying organs. So it is with persons; so it is with places and landscapes. There comes a time when a tree or grove reaches "threescore and ten." Maybe we've kept the fires, bulldozers, chainsaws, and floodwaters at bay, extending a landscape's life expectancy to its version of "fourscore"—be that fifty, one hundred, or five hundred years. But eventually rot or disease or fire or flood will come and make a mockery of our life-support measures. How to let these places that we love, that tell stories of who we are and want to become, live and die with dignity is extremely difficult.

When we've done our best to hold nature and humanity at bay, yet those points of fixity still dissolve in advancing flames, it's okay to mourn. The loss is real and the pain must be acknowledged, for the sweet smell of ponderosa bark is replaced by acrid charcoal. Memories remain, though the deceased is missing. Life will continue, though it has changed. Experiencing grief (and attending to its tasks) over loss of a place is as important as experiencing grief for the loss of a person—whether a friend, a parent, or a spouse. It may not be as intense or ultimately significant; it is as real. And here we pass the fourth cairn of loss.

6 | DRIFT SMOKE

In country not seen in the daylight.
—Watch Out Situation Number 2

You are dust, and to dust you shall return.
—Genesis 3:19

Light drizzle fell as I began down the trail, between granite crosses and thick Gambel oak. Four years after my first visit to Storm King Mountain I had returned, only to be driven from its slopes by the dark underbelly of a thunderstorm. A camera tripod protruded from the top of my backpack. Although death by lightning—upon the ashes of a burn—is about as good a way as any for a firefighter to exit terra firma, I didn't want to tempt fate. Plus, I had yet to visit the Storm King Monument in Glenwood Springs.

Just the day before I was in Missoula. Traveling south, I noticed old fire scars all along the freeway between Montana and Utah. By early evening I was shacked up in a sweltering motel room in Springville, Utah, at the base of the Wasatch Range. In the pink glow of a sun setting behind towering cumulus, I could see the gray skeletons of trees from an old fire above town—confirmation that death still lurks in countless nooks and crannies of the West. The next afternoon I'd arrive where death was realized on July 6, 1994.

Just a few miles southwest of Storm King, and not far off Interstate 70, I passed Battlement Mesa, site of the 1976 Battlement Creek fire, where three firefighters died. While circumstances at Battlement Creek differed from South Canyon, that deaths occurred in such close proximity is at the very least peculiar. Maybe it says something about fires in this area or about the people who fight fires in this area; maybe it says something about both. I'm not sure.

In 1994, when I first saw South Canyon, very little marked the way to the place where fourteen men and women died. A gravel cul-de-sac beneath a southerly ridge off Storm King Mountain was as close as you could get to the fire area in a vehicle, with a cross-country trek on foot from there. Mainly, I orienteered by fresh memories of newscasts showing the smoking main ridge, dotted by yellow tarps under which lay bodies. Today there is a paved parking area, an outhouse, interpretive signs with pictures of the fourteen deceased, a white plastic vase holding walking staffs that hikers can borrow, a metal registration box, and a well-marked, water-barred trail. Along the path are more interpretive signs, culminating in an overlook from which you can see most of the points where the critical events of 1994 occurred. From there to the crosses the trail has been left primitive, marked only by rock cairns. As one sign says, this is to pay "tribute to the firefighters who lost their lives," because the ground on which firefighters work is rugged. I like that, even if the path has become well worn by its many pilgrims.

I wondered if there was too much explanation along the trail, too many signs helping visitors process and make sense of what may never be fully sensible. But this is a community's effort (really two communities' efforts: Glenwood Springs and the wildland fire community) to make meaning, to grieve, and to pay tribute. The signs set the human tragedy in the context of fire ecology, which is an admirable juxtaposition. In the end, I'm not sure if excessive explanation is any more blameworthy than nine riderless horses in a central Oregon parade, in tribute to firefighters who no longer ride horses. And maybe the "excesses" will help ensure that the fatalities are remembered.

Weather and drought conditions probably had more to do with the fire behavior on July 6, 1994, than did fuel buildup and the historic loss of fire on the west slope of the Rockies. Human fallibility on the ground probably had as much to do with the loss of life as did fallible fire policy that risked people's necks for homes built amidst flammable fuels. Would Canyon Creek Estates, to the west of the South Canyon fire, or Glenwood Springs, to the east, have lost even one home had not a single firefighter set foot on the fire's perimeter on July 6? But if no one had set foot on the fire and houses burned, would the public have sat stoically by and accepted the loss (even though virtually no one believes that any house is worth sacrificing one's life over)? Or, perhaps, is sacrifice the wrong metaphor? I've never known a firefighter who would willingly lay down his or her life for some scrap of brush or cedar siding. "Accident" may be a better way to describe their deaths.

If houses had burned, the losses would have been real. If special places had burned, these losses, too, would have been real. Yet even if such places had existed, none of their symbolic values would outweigh the human beings—the valuers—overcome by the fire. Lives were lost, and these losses were real. For fourteen, the subjunctive mood went up in flames.

I left the trailhead at 2:30 in the afternoon. I arrived at the main ridge by 4:00 PM—the same time that, four years earlier, gale-force winds whipped a spotfire into a firefront that within thirteen minutes overtook twelve firefighters, and nine minutes later trapped two more. There were still plenty of black juniper, piñon pine, and Gambel oak snags within the burn's perimeter, but where my first visit negotiated a landscape tinged with white and gray ash sifted over exposed red soil, this time I traversed through shades of green on red.

My first goal was to find the markers for the two helitack crewmen that I failed to locate on my first trip. A co-worker from Prineville had told me about his visit to the spot where these two died. He said that it reminded him of a house fire—victims curled up in some inescapable corner (under a bed, in a closet, up against a wall) where they tried to hide or seek refuge before the smoke and fumes and heat cut off all hope of escape. Browning and Tyler, the two helitack crew members, were likewise hemmed in while escaping: by vertical rock and slippery scree at the head of a draw. Instead of quilted blankets to curl up in under a bed, they tried to cover themselves with metallic fire shelters, but to no avail. Superheated fumes rendered the air boiling poison. I've heard armchair firefighters heap scorn on Browning and Tyler's decision to run upcanyon, the very place where all firefighters are taught not to go because canyons funnel fire like chimneys. But as westerly winds swept fire up over the main ridge, threatening to overtake crews escaping down its east face, these two no doubt thought an end run around the north side of the blowup might lead them to safety. Maybe they were hoping that their helicopter would find them. Undoubtedly, as their world became bracketed by smoke to the south on its way to the east and rock to the north that might or might not become enveloped in smoke, whatever they saw, heard, and felt in their guts led them north.

When I located their crosses, I saw that my co-worker was right: Browning and Tyler had nowhere to go, just vertical red rock obscured by thickening smoke. They made it a long way, a hell of a long way—over a thousand feet from H-2 (helispot number two) on the main ridge. Even though I was sweating and the air was very hot, a chill spasmed across my skin, like when I saw the illuminated flags on the courthouse lawn several years earlier. Who would expect to see crosses in an unnamed ravine where there should be only red sandstone and juniper and sage?

On top of and next to each cross lay mementos left by friends, family, and visitors: a rumpled baseball cap, a pulaski, plastic flowers, a crusty yellow fireshirt, a bottle of beer, beads, embroidered patches from different fire agencies, faded purple ribbons. Back down the main ridge, where twelve other granite crosses had replaced the steel spikes and small brass tags that I saw in 1994, similar mementos surrounded each spot where firefighters spent their last moments of life: photographs, a set of dog tags, handwritten notes sealed in ziplock baggies, an American flag, a medicine wheel from which silver feathers fluttered in the breeze, a small clay angel, a pair of skis planted in the ground, a double-spring steel trap, a hardhat, more purple ribbons.

I photographed the last cross as the light dimmed and mammatus clouds rippled the sky like skeins of ripe salmon eggs. Perhaps I'd gawked long enough. Perhaps I'd spent too much time photographing and not enough time just sitting at each cross pondering why this one? Why did this one die on a hill now lush with Gambel oak regrowth sprouting from the very black skeletons that once appeared dead? It was only fitting to be driven from the mountain by an impending storm, the very phenomenon that began the whole sequence that led to these crosses and my visit to Colorado.

The next morning I ventured to Glenwood Springs. Most of the folks swarming through the town's swank little shops or dipping in the Hotel Colorado's hot springs pool probably had no idea that firefighters died on a ridge just west of town. Part of my reason for visiting Glenwood Springs was to interview residents, to get a feel for how a tragedy like the South Canyon fire has affected their community, even four years after the fact. Bad strategy on my part. Not only do I hate conducting interviews (feeling

a little like a phone solicitor calling at mealtime), but I'd neg-
lected to consider that the tabloids had already been sniffing
around the town's fire hydrants and crapping in other people's
backyards. Luckily, my having worked in Prineville during 1994
helped raise my credibility enough to gain a few minutes with the
Glenwood Springs fire chief, Jim Mason.

It was obvious that Jim was feeling me out as much as I was
picking his brain. He said he had no time for those who sat at a
safe distance critiquing Storm King. "They really fry my ass," he
said. "Mine too," I replied. He also said that he'd turned down
many interviews but would try to answer my questions. I really
only had one question for him: "How has the tragedy changed
the community?" Jim didn't feel like he could speak for the whole
community, though he attempted an answer.

"I'm sure a lot of people look up at the mountain and don't
feel anything," he said. "But every time I look up there, I feel a
hole in my middle." As he said this, he formed a circle with his
hands and placed it over his abdomen.

That was my interview. Having lost all interest in probing
what appeared to be a raw nerve, I diverted the conversation to
my own interest in fire and loss, and my frustration with back-
seat firefighters. We cordially shook hands, and I left. I felt a little
sheepish, certainly intrusive. I think I knew the answer to my
question before ever entering the fire station. There will always
be people in every community who are oblivious to the most severe tragedies in their midst. Of the rest, a large percentage will
grieve for a time but move on and only infrequently dwell on

what's perceived as "negative." These people rarely notice chalky green plaques, tattered flags, and the holes in which flags should be planted that are now filled with rainwater and pine needles. Then there are those who are left with holes in their middle. Maybe the trail up the mountain, and the monument in town, ought to speak for the community. Maybe I shouldn't worry so much about what the community thinks about this tragedy, for the real reason I traveled a thousand miles to get here was more selfish: to reconnect with a place that forever changed how I view fire and my relationship to fire in a land of fire.

Before I left Glenwood Springs, I visited the bronze statue at Two Rivers Park. It includes a smokejumper, a helitack crew-person, and a hotshot, the three facing outward in different directions as if circling the wagons. Centered among them stands a bronze Gambel oak bush. A rock wall encircles the statue, forming a planter box in which wildflowers grow. Affixed to one of the rocks is a small plaque, and next to the plaque is an inset chunk of quartz. The plaque reads:

THE SPLIT QUARTZ GEODE
SYMBOLIZES THE BOND BETWEEN
GLENWOOD SPRINGS, CO, AND
PRINEVILLE, OR.
THE OTHER HALF REMAINS IN PRINEVILLE, OR,
"HOME OF THE HOT SHOT CREW"

It's strange how in a matter of minutes an obscure ridge thrust two small communities into the national limelight, a light that has dimmed, though a light that still glitters in two geode halves a thousand miles apart. A flame that still burns in the memories of hot, smoky July days.

Storm King Mountain receded in my rearview mirror as I passed beneath cumulus on their way to becoming thunderheads, storms that would chase me all the way to Wyoming. As lightning started new fires, I drove past more old burns. In Flaming Gorge National Recreation Area, I spotted a sign that read "Firefighters Memorial." I pulled off to discover a monument dedicated to three firefighters killed on the Cart Creek fire of 1977. I'd never heard of Cart Creek before and wondered how many other monuments like this one are scattered around the country? How many, like this one, were once well known but have slipped into obscurity like so much drift smoke from a cooling fire?

...

Life is tenuous, fragile, contingent, and in constant danger of decay and death. Recognizing this, some so fear death that they try to avoid it at all cost. Others recognize the inevitability of death yet see it, from a religious perspective, as an affront to nature—a result of sin. They embrace a primordial past of Edenic bliss (lost in the "fall" from grace) and a hereafter that literally includes lions lying down with lambs, *Panthera leo* cuddling *Ovis aries.* To help usher in this future kingdom, we may even see it as our moral imperative to replicate that idealized community in the here and now. In this sense ecological restoration amounts to eliminating those unsavory parts of nature that supposedly reflect God's curse on humanity long ago in ancient Mesopotamia. These religious-philosophical sentiments permeate many of our perceptions of the world—never mind that the Eden pictured in the Bible-story books I thumbed through in dentists' and doctors' waiting rooms in my boyhood may never have existed in the past, that no pain-free paradise may ever exist in the future, and that to recreate such conditions in the present might require the loss of many other values that we hold near and dear, as I've suggested in the previous pages. To eliminate all manner of death and decay would require both physical and metaphysical alteration of the world in which we actually live.

On the other hand, not all manner of death and disease should be embraced at all times and at all places. To do so in the human realm would require shunning all achievements of medicine, returning us to an age of truncated life expectancies and protracted, painful deaths. Sometimes losses are better avoided than embraced. Human agency gives us the ability to alter our habitat and surroundings, at times with seemingly few environmental repercussions that destroy other values in any systemic, long-term sense. Sometimes, for our survival, we may be willing to live with such external losses—that is, loss of some values to avoid losing others. Nevertheless, this is no zero-sum game. To lose something, whether a gangrenous appendage or a species, is truly tragic, and there is no way to sugar-coat its demise or glamorize what we've allegedly gained.

A lingering question always remains, though: Was there no other way? Might we have chosen an alternate path that conserved values and either avoided adversely affecting our world or even enhanced our well-being? Here lies the significance of the "precautionary principle," which advocates caution in the face of uncertainty. Is it pure lack of creativity on our part that limits our ability to live sustainably and respectfully upon this earth, to live as lightly as possible on the land rather than always asking how much of some chemical we can dump into our air or water before it becomes toxic to humans, or how many resources we can extract from the earth before species or ecosystems become irreparably damaged? Is lack of creativity an outgrowth of stubborn and unreflective acceptance of tradition? Laziness? Hubris? Infatuation with ever-increasing busyness and hyperactive productivity?[1]

In his essay "Life without Principle," Henry David Thoreau writes: "If a man walk in the woods for love of them half of each day, he is in danger of being regarded as a loafer; but if he spends his whole day as speculator, shearing off those woods and making earth bald before her time, he is esteemed an industrious and enterprising citizen."[2] Over a century and a half later, we remain so enamored of notions of industry and enterprise that shun all manner of loss—be it a drop in the Dow Jones or the decay of a ponderosa pine snag—that we fail to seriously consider how our world, our lives and livelihoods, might be other than they are, how they might be less a burden on our neighbors and our neighborhoods, our fellow living creatures, their habitat and our habitat together.

Living with fire is a matter of choices, a matter of seeing the connection between loss on a personal scale and loss on a landscape scale: in relationship with persons and in relationship to and with the land. If we struggle with these matters in the arena of our lives to which we at least ostensibly assign preeminent value—the lives of other persons—it's no wonder that we struggle with the very same issues when they are more removed from that sphere. Fire may be one of the most dramatic natural phenomena from which these tensions erupt, but the same struggle also subsists within most environmental debates (which really are cultural and existential debates) about value or disvalue, whether of predators, undeveloped lands, uncut forests, ungrazed range, or wilderness. While these issues certainly involve matters of human-centeredness versus intrinsic or inherent value, "male" domination of nature versus "feminine" nurturing, and myriad other factors that have historically separated us from the earth, they are not exclusively the domain of any one factor, just as viewing one cairn of loss in isolation does not explain our relationship with fire. At one and the same time, these issues are much less opaque and much more complex than we might think. The argument that I've been trying to make is that humility and empathy and care are not only core virtues between humans but are also essential virtues in our attitudes and actions toward the earth.[3]

Loss is a tangible and pervasive reality that we deal with every day at a human level but often fail to perceive in our relationship with nature. The challenge before us—vis-à-vis fire and vis-à-vis nature in general—is this: can we see this connection between human loss and loss in nature? Probably not if we cling tenaciously to the belief that all losses are evil in an absolute sense. Probably not if we see nature as entirely other than humans and interhuman relationships. Probably not if we unthinkingly embrace all loss as natural without recognizing how we already distinguish between acceptable and unacceptable losses (in both degree and kind) in our lives. In saying this, I'm not suggesting merely that we adopt a golden mean between embracing and disparaging loss, but rather that we recognize how we already accept and reject some forms of loss, often without realizing it and often without critically reflecting on why we're doing so.

But virtues are not formed in a vacuum; while some modicum of humility, charity, and generosity is essential to even begin the dialogue—with ourselves and with one another—about living with fire, walking the cairns firsthand cannot be replicated at a distance. By walking I mean literally traversing ground: viewing the regenerative effects of fire on land; visiting a firefighter's memorial or, better yet, the slopes where young men and women lost their lives amidst the flames of summer; participating in a prescribed burn or other restoration work; or exploring our sacred groves, meditating on whether they are more important if retained as they are or allowed to die a natural death, even if it be in our lifetime and even if it be to wildfire. The environmental philosopher Eric Higgs identifies such grassroots practices—"focal practices" as he calls them—as critical components of ecological restoration:

The meaning of ecological restoration has evolved from a singular focus on bringing back ecological integrity to a recognition that both the process and product of restoration can have salutary benefits for people—bringing people together in the act of restoration builds community, and the restoration projects themselves often offer educational, recreational, and scientific value. . . . Not only are there instrumental benefits from restoring places, but also presumably the very goal of restoration ought to be one of cultural as well as ecological restoration. Thus, what is being restored encompasses cultural beliefs and practices along with ecological processes, structures, and patterns.[4]

Again, we must wrestle with the issue of scale. Increased professionalization and specialization in natural-resource management has distanced much of the American public from tangible acts of care, much as professionalization in the medical profession has distanced many from the dying process.[5] Nevertheless, palliative care among humans is often on a very different scale than palliative, or restorative, care for nature. To clean up a toxic waste dump, or even to manage fire on a landscape scale, may be beyond the skill and logistical scope of those of us who simply want to pull on some gloves and lend a hand. However, this should not be an excuse for relegating all hands-on work of natural-resource management and restoration to professionals, who may or may not be as skilled or as cognizant of their own biases as we might hope. When it comes to logistics, efficiency is not the only value at stake, and sometimes for the sake of our individual and collective physical, mental, and spiritual well-being we may need to sacrifice our desire to quickly and painlessly allow someone else to heal the land that we and our forebears have damaged. Orienteering the cairns cannot be done by proxy. In traversing them firsthand, we might catch a glimpse of how loss permeates our world, what that has meant for us in the past, and what that might mean for us in the future.

That's the optimist in me speaking. Unfortunately, while there is something intuitively appealing about close association with the land being a necessary condition for understanding fire and loss, I don't believe that such "ruralism" is either a necessary or a sufficient condition to viewing the cairns in a way that engenders understanding, respect, and humility. This is not to say that focal practices don't help in the formation of a land ethic. Still, there are too many examples of individuals who have lived close to the land (maybe even having engaged fire) who are unable or unwilling to recognize values in nature, or the cairns of loss, other than those that are purely utilitarian. "Long-term tenure," writes the conservation biologist Michael E. Soulé, "does not necessarily guarantee a benign attitude toward biodiversity or even toward the natural resources on which long-term economic welfare depends. Witness the destruction of soils, old-growth forests, and fisheries in the United States, often by local people who have been exploiting the resource for many generations."[6]

Trying to restore certain losses may be difficult, if not impossible. Thousands of years of kindling fires have nudged landscapes down paths that may never be retraced. According to Nancy Langston, "After we interfere with a [forest] community, that community's history proceeds along paths quite different from those it would have taken without our interference. Each disturbance, whether human or natural, represents a branch in the path of forest history, and each action takes the forest in a slightly different direction. We cannot simply backtrack to a time before some particular decision we now regret, because so many additional changes have radiated out from that original action."[7]

Every time we enter fire's environment, we set foot onto a landscape storied by human and nonhuman forces, a stream of history whose upper reaches can never be fully portaged by ecological restoration or land management. It's difficult, if not impossible, to know exactly how the West *would* have looked if people had never brought fire between ice into a land that burned. Even if we could, is that how the land ought to look now? Even if that's how we would like the land to look, is it possible? Probably not, given the oscillations of climate and land over millennia. It may not even be possible to reclaim the landscape crafted by these peoples; if we can, it's not at all clear why we should. Is our difficulty in honestly answering these questions rooted in our refusal to follow the cairns, or do we fail to understand the cairns as loss?

The cairns of loss can be dim or blinding. Like the convection columns from adjacent forest fires, they're able to influence each other and, at times, even overtake each other, becoming one fire clawing through the atmosphere, sucking in air, drawing smaller fires toward its core. Hence, one loss may contribute to another loss, and one may be cataclysmic. The existence of two crosses at the head of a ravine where there shouldn't be crosses opens a permanent chasm in the land of the living.

The cairns are distinct—like four flickering mounds in the darkness between sky and ground—but they are also inseparable. To craft a sustainable, moral relationship with this land we call the West, or any land that burns, we must pass each of these fires, lingering for a while in its presence to understand the depth of its grief yet remaining mindful of the other cairns marking from whence we came and to where we are headed. In some cases rebirth might follow death, but not always. Even if we know that we'll die and that death is but one part of life, we still must struggle to live in a world that dies, a world that burns and sometimes needs to burn.

• • •

The charcoal smeared black onto my palms. I wanted to feel an old fire, and by caressing the face of the tilted black snag, I could. By pressing my nose against its twisted, turtle-shelled surface, I could smell forty-nine-year-old smoke, the same smoke that Robert Jansson spent his whole life trying to forget.

On the last day of the summer tour-boat season, my wife and I caught a shuttle from the Gates of the Mountains Boat Club to Meriwether Campground, the trailhead into Mann Gulch. In June 1994 all I could think about was planning a filming expedition into Mann Gulch. By July of that summer, the trailhead at Meriwether was the last thing on my mind, and it would stay that way for years to come. But now it was time to finish the journey that I had once drawn on a map, of winds moving upcanyon and of life moving toward death.

Two-thirds of the way up a zigzagging path, we passed into the southern edge of the burn—near a black snag that smelled of fire. At the top of the ridge separating Meriwether Canyon and Mann Gulch, we got our first glimpse of the slope on which eleven men died and two others were severely burned. The gulch looked familiar: dry, hot, steep, and rocky. It could just as easily been named Thirtymile, Macks, Jones, Pine Hollow, Smith, or Little Ferry. In Oregon. Along the breaks of the Deschutes or John Day Rivers. Or a thousand other places in the West.

The north side of the gulch was mainly just grass intermixed with crunchy dry balsam root and white concrete crosses. Because they're rooted on a hot, south-facing slope, it may be centuries, if ever, before these crosses are overshadowed by vegetation. A few snags still balance vertically, though most are prostrate and barely visible. Prior to the fire, stringers of timber descended into the canyon, yet in forty-nine years few new trees have grown and those few are still small. In contrast, the north-facing slope (on the south side of Mann Gulch) is peppered with young pine and fir: a testament to cooler, moister soils.

In 1997 two-foot-tall granite obelisks were placed next to each of the deteriorating crosses. It looks out of balance having both markers just a few feet apart. I suppose it's an attempt to add permanence to what was otherwise a high-maintenance situation, concrete markers that fared poorly on a harsh Montana slope. I'm not sure if it was intentional, but there is an odd tension between the crosses and the pillars: one an obvious religious symbol associated with death, the other a generic object, a vertical name on a pillar of stone. I wondered if it was a deliberate attempt to divest these names, these deaths, of religious connotations. Did the Helena National Forest and Missoula smokejumpers want a clean break between church and state? Or, more likely, was it a more respectful recognition of the lives of those young firefighters who were not of the Christian faith? Whatever the answer, when the last cross crumples during spring thaw, mingling with the white shale that everywhere covers the ground, decades of continuity will collapse with it.

We had time to visit only a handful of crosses before backtracking to the boat landing. As at Storm King, I snapped pictures of each marker I visited. Also as at Storm King, clouds thickened and turned black as we began our retreat.

Lightning crackled through the inky sky as we crossed the divide back into Meriwether Canyon. The thunderhead—like a rainbow but more ambiguous—was a sign: a sign that fire shall not depart the earth anytime soon and that when fires start and burn, losses are inevitable. As Norman Maclean wrote, "the terror of the universe has not yet fossilized and the universe has not run out of blowups."[8] Nor, I might add, is it about to anytime soon.

Someday I'll return to Mann Gulch and Storm King Mountain, to visit each cross and read each name, to sit, to linger, and to rub my hands over peeling black bark. To watch the breeze sway the branches of fresh Gambel oak and adolescent pine.

NOTES

INTRODUCTION

The epigraph is from Sigmund Freud, in *Letters of Sigmund Freud,* ed. E. L. Freud, trans. Tania and James Stern (New York: Basic, 1961), 386.

1. Keith Clark and Lowell Tiller, *Terrible Trail: The Meek Cutoff, 1845* (Bend, OR: Maverick, 1993), 53.

2. Nancy Langston, *Forest Dreams, Forest Nightmares: The Paradox of Old Growth in the Inland West* (Seattle: University of Washington Press, 1995), 291. On attitudes toward human loss, see Elizabeth Kübler-Ross's classic work *On Death and Dying* (New York: Macmillan, 1969).

3. J. William Worden, *Grief Counseling and Grief Therapy: A Handbook for the Mental Health Practitioner,* 2d ed. (New York: Springer, 1991), 10–18. Also see Therese A. Rando, *Grieving: How to Go On Living When Someone You Love Dies* (Lexington, MA: Lexington Books, 1988), 226–60.

4. Rando, *Grieving,* 19–24.

5. Kenneth J. Doka, preface to *Disenfranchised Grief: New Directions, Challenges, and Strategies for Practice,* ed. Kenneth J. Doka (Champaign, IL: Research Press, 2002), xiii; Rando, *Grieving,* 57–61. On loss relative to pets, see Barbara Meyers, "Disenfranchised Grief and the Loss of an Animal Companion," in *Disenfranchised Grief,* ed. Doka, 251–64.

6. Stephen J. Pyne, *Fire in America: A Cultural History of Wildland and Rural Fire* (Princeton, NJ: Princeton University Press, 1982), 44.

1. WINDS

The epigraphs are from the Revised Standard Version of the Bible and Norman Maclean, *Young Men and Fire* (Chicago: University of Chicago Press, 1992), 132–33.

1. Meriwether Lewis, journal entry for "Friday July 19th 1805," in *April 7–July 27, 1805*, vol. 4 of *The Journals of the Lewis and Clark Expedition*, ed. Gary E. Moulton (Lincoln: University of Nebraska Press, 1987), 403.

2. Sandy Dunbar, quoted in Michelle Schaner, "Storm King, Three Years Later: A Day to Remember, a Day to Pay Tribute," *Glenwood (Colo.) Post*, 7 July 1997.

2. SLOW SMOTHER | LOSS OF FIRE

The epigraphs are from Gerald G. Alquist, "Researchers Will Attempt to Turn Tables on Nature," *Missoula Sentinel*, 21 June 1953; and Henry T. Lewis, *A Time for Burning*, Boreal Institute for Northern Studies, Occasional Publication 17 (Edmonton: University of Alberta, 1982), 1.

1. E. James Dixon, *Quest for the Origins of the First Americans* (Albuquerque: University of New Mexico Press, 1993).

2. Cathy W. Barnosky, Patricia M. Anderson, and Patrick J. Bartlein, "The Northwestern U.S. during Deglaciation: Vegetational History and Paleoclimatic Implications," in *North America and Adjacent Oceans during the Last Glaciation*, Geology of North America, vol. K-3, ed. W. F. Ruddiman and H. E. Wright Jr. (Boulder, CO: Geological Society of America, 1987), 289; Linda Brubaker, "Vegetation History and Anticipating Future Vegetation Change," in *Ecosystem Management for Parks and Wilderness*, ed. James K. Agee and Darryll R. Johnson (Seattle: University of Washington Press, 1988), 47.

3. James B. Griffin, "The Origin and Dispersion of American Indians in

North America," in *The First Americans: Origins, Affinities, and Adaptations*, ed. William S. Laughlin and Albert B. Harper (New York: Gustav Fischer, 1979), 49; Dixon, *Quest*, 123 (see 98–101, 114, for evidence regarding significantly earlier human occupation of the Americas).

4. William G. Robbins and Donald W. Wolf, *Landscape and the Intermontane Northwest: An Environmental History*, General Technical Report PNW-GTR-319 (Portland, OR: U.S. Department of Agriculture, Forest Service, Pacific Northwest Research Station, 1994), 3. See also Charles L. Matsch, *North America and the Great Ice Age* (New York: McGraw-Hill, 1976), 117, and Charles G. Johnson Jr. et al., *Biotic and Abiotic Processes of Eastside Ecosystems: The Effects of Management on Plant and Community Ecology, and on Stand and Landscape Vegetation Dynamics*, General Technical Report PNW-GTR-322 (Portland, OR: U.S. Department of Agriculture, Forest Service, Pacific Northwest Research Station, 1994), 28.

5. Paul Alaback, University of Montana School of Forestry, personal communication, 4 January 1999.

6. Brubaker, "Vegetation History," 44; Pyne, *Fire in America*, 491.

7. Lewis, *A Time for Burning*, 12, discusses northern Alberta's indigenous peoples' use of fire to control vegetative succession.

8. Pyne, *Fire in America*, 491–93; Brubaker, "Vegetation History," 41. For a good discussion of Clementian theory related to Oregon's Blue Mountains, see Langston, *Forest Dreams, Forest Nightmares*, 37, 125–28, 132–33, 213–14. Also regarding Clements, see Donald Worster, *Nature's Economy: A History of Ecological Ideas*, 2d ed. (New York: Cambridge University Press, 1994), 205–20.

9. See Robbins and Wolf, *Landscape and the Intermontane Northwest*, 2; Dean A. Shinn, "Historical Perspectives on Range Burning in the Inland Pacific Northwest," *Journal of Range Management* 33, no. 6 (1980): 415–23; Charles E. Kay, "Aboriginal Overkill and Native Burning: Implications for

Modern Ecosystem Management," *Western Journal of Applied Forestry* 10, no. 4 (1995): 121–26; and Alston Chase, *Playing God in Yellowstone: The Destruction of America's First National Park* (San Diego: Harcourt Brace Jovanovich, 1987), 97ff.

10. Glacial Lake Great Falls may already have drained by the time humans entered northern Montana, but they still would have passed near its location.

11. Steve Arno, Intermountain Fire Sciences Laboratory, personal communication, 22 October 1998.

12. Regarding evolutionary adaptations to fire, see George E. Howe, "The Evolutionary Role of Wildfire in the Northern Rockies and Implications for Resource Managers," in *Proceedings—Tall Timbers Fire Ecology Conference and Fire and Land Management Symposium, No. 14, 8–10 October 1974* (Tallahassee: Tall Timbers Research Station, 1976), 257–65; Stephen F. Arno and Steven Allison-Bunnell, *Flames in Our Forest: Disaster or Renewal?* (Washington, DC: Island Press, 2002), 51–64; and James K. Agee, *Fire and Weather Disturbance in Terrestrial Ecosystems of the Eastern Cascades,* General Technical Report PNW-GTR-320 (Portland, OR: U.S. Department of Agriculture, Forest Service, Pacific Northwest Research Station, 1994), 5. Regarding fire in Yellowstone National Park and the greater Yellowstone ecosystem, see William H. Romme and Don G. Despain, "Historical Perspective on the Yellowstone Fires of 1988: A Reconstruction of Prehistoric Fire History Reveals That Comparable Fires Occurred in the Early 1700s," *Bioscience* 39, no. 10 (1989): 695–99, and William H. Romme and Don G. Despain, "Long History of Fire in the Greater Yellowstone Ecosystem," *Western Wildlands: A Natural Resource Journal* 15 (Summer 1989): 10–17.

13. For a global perspective of fire's effects on biota, see Stephen J. Pyne, *World Fire: The Culture of Fire on Earth* (New York: Henry Holt, 1995).

14. Pyne, *Fire in America*, 81.

15. Lewis, *A Time for Burning*, 4ff.; Henry T. Lewis, "Why Indians Burned: Specific versus General Reasons," in *Proceedings—Symposium and Workshop on Wilderness Fire, Missoula, Montana, November 15–18, 1983*, General Technical Report INT-GTR-182 (Ogden, UT: U.S. Department of Agriculture, Forest Service, Intermountain Forest and Range Experiment Station, 1985), 76; Gerald W. Williams, "American Indian Use of Fire in Ecosystems: Thousands of Years of Managing Landscapes," revision of a paper presented at the annual meeting of the American Ecological Society, Albuquerque, NM, August 1997 (Portland, OR: U.S. Department of Agriculture, Forest Service, Pacific Northwest Region, 1997, photocopy), 2.

16. Pyne, *Fire in America*, 81. Also see C. Mark Cowell, "Ecological Restoration and Environmental Ethics," *Environmental Ethics* 15 (Spring 1993): 29 n. 53, for a similar point on Native Americans.

17. Chase, *Playing God in Yellowstone*, 97.

18. Michael Williams, *Americans and Their Forests: A Historical Geography* (New York: Cambridge University Press, 1989), 33; Henry F. Dobyns, *Their Number Become Thinned: Native American Population Dynamics in Eastern North America* (Knoxville: University of Tennessee Press, 1983); Kay, "Aboriginal Overkill and Native Burning," 125. See Eugene S. Hunn with James Selam and Family, *Nch'i-Wána, "The Big River": Mid-Columbia Indians and Their Land* (Seattle: University of Washington Press, 1990), 27–32, regarding the population crash of Columbia Plateau tribes, and Gerald Williams, "American Indian Use of Fire," 5, regarding depopulation of Oregon's Willamette Valley.

19. Peter J. Mehringer Jr., Stephen F. Arno, and Kenneth L. Petersen, "Postglacial History of Lost Trail Pass Bog, Bitterroot Mountains, Montana," *Arctic and Alpine Research* 9, no. 4 (1977): 345–68.

20. Ibid., 366. Regarding Indian tribes in northwest Montana, see Carling I. Malouf, "Flathead and Pend d'Oreille," in *Handbook of North American Indians*, ed. William C. Sturtevant, vol. 12, *Plateau*, ed. Deward E. Walker Jr. (Washington, DC: Smithsonian Institution, 1998), 297–312.

21. Thomas R. Vale, "The Myth of the Humanized Landscape: An Example from Yosemite National Park," *Natural Areas Journal* 18, no. 3 (1998): 234, 232. Also see Shepard Krech III, *The Ecological Indian: Myth and History* (New York: W. W. Norton, 1999), 110.

22. Stephen W. Barrett, "Relationship of Indian-Caused Fires to the Ecology of Western Montana Forests" (master's thesis, University of Montana, 1981). Also see Stephen F. Arno, Helen Y. Smith, and Michael A. Krebs, *Old Growth Ponderosa Pine and Western Larch Stand Structures: Influences of Pre-1900 Fires and Fire Exclusion*, Research Paper INT-RP-495 (Portland, OR: U.S. Department of Agriculture, Forest Service, Intermountain Research Station, 1997), esp. pp. 14 and 17–19.

23. For artistic representations of fire in the American West of the nineteenth century, see George Catlin's *Prairie Meadows Burning* (1832) and *Indian Family Alarmed at Approach of a Prairie Fire* (1832), in Royal B. Hassrick, *The George Catlin Book of American Indians* (New York: Watson-Guptill, 1977), 175, 186, and *Prairie Bluffs Burning*, in Harold McCracken, *George Catlin and the Old Frontier* (New York: Bonanza Books, 1959), 145; Alfred Jacob Miller's *Prairie on Fire*, in Marvin C. Ross, *The West of Alfred Jacob Miller* (Norman: University of Oklahoma Press, 1968), 198; Paul Kane's *A Prairie on Fire* (1846), in J. Russell Harper, *Paul Kane's Frontier* (Austin: University of Texas Press, 1971), 210; Charles Wimar's *Buffalo Crossing the Yellowstone*, in Royal B. Hassrick, *The Colorful Story of the American West* (London: Octopus Books, 1975), 10–11; Nicolas Point's *The Village of Sacred Heart Viewed from the West, The Village of Sacred Heart Seen from the North*, and *The Best Time to Shoot Deer Was in the Autumn just*

before Mating Season, in *Wilderness Kingdom: Indian Life in the Rocky Mountains: 1840–1847, The Journals and Paintings of Nicolas Point, S.J.,* trans. Joseph P. Donnelly (Chicago: Loyola University Press, 1967), 76–77, 83; Currier & Ives lithographs *Life on the Prairie: The Trapper's Defense—"Fire Fight Fire"* (1862), and *Prairie Fires of the Great West* (1871), in *Currier & Ives: Chronicles of America,* ed. John Lowell Pratt (Maplewood, NJ: Hammond, 1968), 100, 140; and Frederic Remington's *The Grass Fire* (1908), in Peter H. Hassrick, *Frederic Remington: Paintings, Drawings, and Sculpture in the Amon Carter Museum and the Sid W. Richardson Foundation Collections* (New York: Harry N. Abrams, 1973), 163.

24. John Wesley Powell, *Report on the Lands of the Arid Region of the United States, With a More Detailed Account of the Lands of Utah,* 2d ed.(Washington, DC: Government Printing Office, 1879), 17.

25. See, for instance, Pyne, *Fire in America,* 54 and 143ff.

26. Ibid., 105, and for an extensive discussion of the "light-burning controversy," 100–22.

27. Warren E. Coman, "Did the Indian Protect the Forest?" *Pacific Monthly,* September 1911, 300.

28. G. M. Homans, cited in "Random Talk on Forest Fires," no author given, *American Forestry,* November 1910, 669; E. Deckert, "Forest Fires in North America: A German View," trans. George Wetmore Colles, *American Forestry,* May 1911, 277.

29. Langston, *Forest Dreams, Forest Nightmares,* 46; Pyne, *Fire in America,* 81–83; Kay, "Aboriginal Overkill and Native Burning," 121.

30. For a number of examples of contemporary Native American fire use, see Thomas C. Blackburn and Kat Anderson, eds., *Before the Wilderness: Environmental Management by Native Californians* (Menlo Park, CA: Ballena Press, 1993).

31. Henry T. Lewis, "Patterns of Indian Burning in California: Ecology and Ethnohistory," in *Before the Wilderness,* ed. Blackburn and Anderson, 87–88.

32. Lewis, "Why Indians Burned," 76.

33. Barrett, "Relationship of Indian-Caused Fires," 116ff.; Stephen W. Barrett and Stephen F. Arno, "Indian Fires as an Ecological Influence in the Northern Rockies," *Journal of Forestry,* October 1982, 647–51; Leslie M. Johnson Gottesfeld, "Aboriginal Burning for Vegetation Management in Northwest British Columbia," *Human Ecology,* June 1994; George E. Gruell, "Indian Fires in the Interior West: A Widespread Influence," in *Proceedings—Symposium and Workshop on Wilderness Fire, Missoula, Montana, November 15–18, 1983,* General Technical Report INT-GTR-182 (Ogden, UT: U.S. Department of Agriculture, Forest Service, Intermountain Forest and Range Experiment Station, April 1985), 69–71; Lewis, "Why Indians Burned," 75–79; Pyne, *World Fire,* 303–308; Gerald W. Williams, "References on the American Indian Use of Fire in Ecosystems" (Portland, OR: U.S. Department of Agriculture, Forest Service Pacific Northwest Region, photocopy), 3–4; Williams, "American Indian Use of Fire," 2.

34. Lewis, "Why Indians Burned," 75, 77.

35. Krech, *Ecological Indian,* 110–11.

36. Dennis Martinez, "Indigenous Patterns of Burning" paper presented at the annual meeting of the Society for Ecological Restoration, Austin, Tex., September 1998; Omar C. Stewart, "Fire as the First Great Force Employed by Man," in *Man's Role in Changing the Face of the Earth,* ed. William L. Thomas (Chicago: University of Chicago Press, 1956), 125; Paul Alaback, personal communication, 4 January 1999; Steve Arno, personal communication, 17 December 1998.

37. Regarding other factors, besides the loss of indigenous people's use of fire, that have contributed to the loss of fire in the American West, see

Stephen W. Barrett, "What to Do about the Fire Exclusion Problem," *Wildfire*, March 1999, 12, and Michael E. Soulé, "The Social Siege of Nature," in *Reinventing Nature? Responses to Postmodern Deconstruction*, ed. Michael E. Soulé and Gary Lease (Washington, DC: Island Press, 1995), 158–61.

38. Chase, *Playing God in Yellowstone*, 115.

39. For instance, see Aldo Leopold, "Grass, Brush, Timber, and Fire in Southern Arizona," *Journal of Forestry*, October 1924, 2–3.

3. LEARNING TO REMEMBER | LOSS OF LIFE

The epigraphs are from Joe Halm, "Gallant Joe Halm Tells His Dramatic Experience," *Montana: The Magazine of Western History* 10, no. 4 (1960): 58; Maclean, *Young Men and Fire*, 252; and Marc Racicot to the Editor, *Glenwood (Colo.) Post*, 7 July 1995.

1. Thaddeus A. Roe, quoted in Stan Cohen and Don Miller, *The Big Burn: The Northwest's Forest Fire of 1910* (Missoula, MT: Pictorial Histories, 1978), 59.

2. Maclean, *Young Men and Fire*, 92.

3. George Catlin, *Letters and Notes on the Manners, Customs, and Conditions of the North American Indians*, vol. 2 (1841; reprint, New York: Dover, 1973), 17.

4. Richard Manning, "The Failure of Literature," in *Northern Lights: A Selection of New Writing from the American West*, ed. Deborah Clow and Donald Snow (New York: Vintage Books, 1994), 72.

5. [U.S. Forest Service document.] *Montana: The Magazine of Western History* 10, no. 3 (1960): 58.

6. Arno and Allison-Bunnell, *Flames in Our Forest*, 20–21, 33–34.

7. Jim Bird, quoted in Robert J. Gates, "Grass Valley Fire Contained," *The Dalles (Ore.) Daily Chronicle,* 13 July 1994.

8. Søren Kierkegaard, "The Attack upon 'Christendom,'" in *A Kierkegaard Anthology,* ed. Robert Bretall (New York: Modern Library, 1946), 448–49.

9. Edward C. Pulaski, "Surrounded by Forest Fires: My Most Exciting Experience as a Forest Ranger," *American Forestry,* August 1923, 486.

10. F. A. Silcox, "How the Fires Were Fought," *American Forestry,* November 1910, 638.

11. National Wildfire Coordinating Group, *Historical Wildland Fire-fighter Fatalities, 1910–1996,* 2d ed., PMS 822/NFES 1849 (N.p.: U.S. Department of Agriculture, U.S. Department of the Interior, and the National Association of State Foresters, 1997).

12. E. B. Fussell, "Idaho's Thirty Days' War," *Collier's Weekly,* 24 September 1910, 16, 26–28.

13. Paul R. Greever, "Dedication Address—Blackwater Memorial," in the program for the "Dedication Service: Blackwater Firefighters Memorial and Clayton Gulch Marker, Shoshone National Forest, August 20, 1939," U.S. Department of Agriculture, Forest Service, 7–8.

14. For good treatments of Maclean's struggle to write what became *Young Men and Fire,* see O. Alan Weltzien's "Norman Maclean and Laird Robinson: A Tale of Two Research Partners," *Montana: The Magazine of Western History* 45, no. 1 (1995): 46–55 and "The Two Lives of Norman Maclean and the Text of Fire in *Young Men and Fire,*" *Western American Literature,* May 1994, 3–24.

15. Maclean, *Young Men and Fire,* 300.

16. Ecclesiastes 1:12–14, 17, Revised Standard Version.

17. Peter A. Angeles, *Dictionary of Philosophy* (New York: Barnes and Noble Books, 1981), 296.

18. Laurence Perrine, *Literature: Structure, Sound, and Sense,* 4th ed. (New York: Harcourt Brace Jovanovich, 1983), 1052–55.

19. Maclean, *Young Men and Fire,* 29.

20. Ibid., 37.

21. Ibid., 46; see p. 38 for Maclean's description of tragedy as a "filled-in" story.

22. Manning, "Failure of Literature," 68, 73.

23. Maclean, *Young Men and Fire,* 296. For a similar critique of Manning, see David Toole, in *Waiting for Godot in Sarajevo: Theological Reflections on Nihilism, Tragedy, and Apocalypse* (Boulder, CO: Westview Press, 1998), 122–23.

24. Maclean, *Young Men and Fire,* 256.

25. Lois Jansson, "Have You Ever Stopped to Wonder?" unpublished autobiography (June 1965), 13, on file with David Turner, public affairs officer, Helena National Forest. Quotations from Lois Jansson's autobiography can also be found in David Turner's *The Thirteenth Fire: The Story of Montana's Mann Gulch Fire* (Helena, MT: Helena National Forest, 1999).

26. Jansson, "Have You Ever Stopped to Wonder?" 46–47.

4. WINTER FEED | LOSS OF LIVELIHOOD

The epigraphs are from Cordia Sloan Duke and Joe B. Frantz, *6,000 Miles of Fence: Life on the XIT Ranch of Texas* (Austin: University of Texas Press, 1961), 59; and U.S. Department of the Interior, Bureau of Land Management, *1961 Fire Plan for the Prineville Grazing District* (Prineville, OR: U.S. Department of the Interior, Bureau of Land Management, Prineville District, ca. 1961).

1. Aldo Leopold, *A Sand County Almanac and Sketches Here and There* (New York: Oxford University Press, 1949), 132.

2. Ibid., 129.

3. I first saw the phrase "mountain time" in Bryan G. Norton's *Toward Unity among Environmentalists* (New York: Oxford University Press, 1991), 146.

4. Richard Manning makes a similar point in "Failure of Literature," 74.

5. Langston, *Forest Dreams, Forest Nightmares,* 5. On farming as an ecological process, see Darin Allen Saul, "Restoring Culture and Nature: Land Use Ecology in the Palouse River Watershed" (Ph.D. diss., Washington State University, 1996), 49.

6. Lewis, "Why Indians Burned," 77. For similar examples from Australia and Tasmania, see Stephen J. Pyne, *Burning Bush: A Fire History of Australia* (New York: Henry Holt, 1991), 95, 97.

7. Barrett, "Relationship of Indian-Caused Fires to the Ecology of Western Montana Forests," 31; Lewis, *A Time for Burning,* 38.

8. Maclean, *Young Men and Fire,* 69–71. For a lengthier discussion of the aesthetic dimensions of fire in general, and wildfire in particular, see David J. Strohmaier, *The Seasons of Fire: Reflections on Fire in the West* (Reno: University of Nevada Press, 2001).

5. THREESCORE AND TEN | LOSS OF PLACE

1. Marybeth Lorbiecki, *Aldo Leopold: A Fierce Green Fire* (Helena, MT: Falcon, 1996), 172, 178–79. Regarding Leopold and fire, see ibid., 167–68, and Curt Meine, *Aldo Leopold: His Life and Work* (Madison: University of Wisconsin Press, 1988), 222–23.

2. Lorbiecki, *Aldo Leopold,* 178–79; Meine, *Aldo Leopold,* 519–20.

3. Leopold, *Sand County Almanac,* 72.

4. Psalms 90:10, Revised Standard Version.

5. Robert Elliot, "Faking Nature," *Inquiry* 25 (1982): 81–93. Similarly, see Eric Katz, "Restoration and Redesign: The Ethical Significance of Human Intervention in Nature," *Restoration and Management Notes* 9 (Winter 1991): 90–96.

6. For compelling examples of repeat photography's ability to demonstrate landscapes' change over time, see George E. Gruell, *Fire in Sierra Nevada Forests: A Photographic Interpretation of Ecological Change since 1849* (Missoula, MT: Mountain Press, 2001); and Eric Higgs, *Nature by Design: People, Natural Process, and Ecological Restoration* (Cambridge, MA: MIT Press, 2003), 132–44. For a discussion of the biases of repeat photography, see Norman L. Christensen, "Succession and Natural Disturbance: Paradigms, Problems, and Preservation of Natural Ecosystems," in *Ecosystem Management for Parks and Wilderness,* ed. Agee and Johnson, 79.

7. Mike Hillis, quoted in Sherry Devlin, "Missoula Foresters Want to Log and Burn the Young to Save the Old," *Missoulian* (Missoula, MT), 22 October 1998.

8. Langston, *Forest Dreams, Forest Nightmares,* 259. On the question of restoring presettlement landscapes, see Saul, "Restoring Culture and Nature," 119, and Krech, *Ecological Indian,* 101–22.

9. Regarding our affinities for certain types of landscapes, see Barrett, "Relationship of Indian-Caused Fires to the Ecology of Western Montana Forests,"119; Edward O. Wilson, *Biophilia* (Cambridge, MA: Harvard University Press, 1984); and David M. Graber, "Resolute Biocentrism: The Dilemma of Wilderness in National Parks," in *Reinventing Nature?* ed. Soulé and Lease, 126.

10. Keith H. Basso, *Wisdom Sits in Places* (Albuquerque: University of New Mexico Press, 1996), 63.

11. Ibid., xiii–xiv.

12. See, for instance, Terri Field, "Caring Relationships with Natural and Artificial Environments," *Environmental Ethics* 17 (Fall 1995): 307–20.

13. Basso, *Wisdom Sits in Places,* 7. On this issue of memory and identity, also see Albert Borgmann, *Crossing the Postmodern Divide* (Chicago: University of Chicago Press, 1993), 106–109.

14. Wendell Berry, *Home Economics* (New York: North Point Press, 1987), 17.

15. Gary Snyder, "The Place, the Region, and the Commons," in *Environmental Philosophy: From Animal Rights to Radical Ecology,* ed. Michael E. Zimmerman et al., 2d ed. (Upper Saddle River, NJ: Prentice Hall, 1998), 442.

16. For a description of the National Park Service's attempt to manage Yellowstone National Park for primarily scenic and recreational, as opposed to ecological, values, see Norton, *Toward Unity among Environmentalists,* 158–62.

17. Robert Marshall, "Mountain Ablaze," *Nature,* June–July 1953, Forest Service Reprint, 4, quoted in Pyne, *Fire in America,* 188.

18. Leopold, *Sand County Almanac,* 141; Berry, *Home Economics,* 17. Holmes Rolston, in "Valuing Wildlands," *Environmental Ethics* 7, no. 1 (1985): 28–29, notes cultural and historical values present in wildlands.

6. DRIFT SMOKE

1. Borgmann, *Crossing the Postmodern Divide,* 98–102.

2. Henry David Thoreau, "Life without Principle," in *The Major Essays of Henry David Thoreau,* ed. Richard Dillman (Albany, NY: Whitston, 2001), 114.

3. See William Kittredge, *The Nature of Generosity* (New York: Alfred A. Knopf, 2000).

4. Higgs, *Nature by Design,* 236–37. Albert Borgmann, in *Crossing the Postmodern Divide,* 116–47, also presents an excellent discussion of focal practices and the importance of communal celebration.

5. Lynne Ann DeSpelder and Albert Lee Strickland, *The Last Dance: Encountering Death and Dying,* 6th ed. (New York: McGraw-Hill Higher Education, 2002), 6, 57.

6. Soulé, "Social Siege of Nature," 158.

7. Langston, *Forest Dreams, Forest Nightmares,* 39. Also see Pyne, *Fire in America,* 17–18; Pyne, *World Fire,* 324; and Dan Flores, *The Natural West: Environmental History in the Great Plains and Rocky Mountains* (Norman: University of Oklahoma Press, 2001), 183–99.

8. Maclean, *Young Men and Fire,* 46.

BIBLIOGRAPHY

Agee, James K. *Fire and Weather Disturbance in Terrestrial Ecosystems of the Eastern Cascades.* General Technical Report PNW-GTR-320. Portland, OR: U.S. Department of Agriculture, Forest Service, Pacific Northwest Research Station, 1994.

Agee, James K., and Darryll R. Johnson, eds. *Ecosystem Management for Parks and Wilderness.* Seattle: University of Washington Press, 1988.

Alquist, Gerald G. "Researchers Will Attempt to Turn Tables on Nature," *Missoula Sentinel,* 21 June 1953.

Angeles, Peter A. *Dictionary of Philosophy,* 296. New York: Barnes and Noble Books, 1981.

Arno, Stephen F., and Steven Allison-Bunnell. *Flames in Our Forest: Disaster or Renewal?* Washington, DC: Island Press, 2002.

Arno, Stephen F., Helen Y. Smith, and Michael A. Krebs. *Old Growth Ponderosa Pine and Western Larch Stand Structures: Influences of Pre-1900 Fires and Fire Exclusion.* Research Paper INT-RP-495. Ogden, UT: U.S. Department of Agriculture, Forest Service, Intermountain Research Station, 1997.

Barnosky, Cathy W., Patricia M. Anderson, and Patrick J. Bartlein. "The Northwestern U.S. during Deglaciation: Vegetational History and Paleoclimatic Implications." In *North America and Adjacent Oceans during the Last Glaciation.* Geology of North America, vol. K-3, edited by W. F. Ruddiman and H. E. Wright Jr., 289–321. Boulder, CO: Geological Society of America, 1987.

Barrett, Stephen W. "Relationship of Indian-Caused Fires to the Ecology of Western Montana Forests." Master's thesis, University of Montana, 1981.

———. "What to Do about the Fire Exclusion Problem." *Wildfire,* March 1999, 12–14.

Barrett, Stephen W., and Stephen F. Arno. "Indian Fires as an Ecological Influence in the Northern Rockies." *Journal of Forestry,* October 1982, 647–51.

Basso, Keith H. *Wisdom Sits in Places.* Albuquerque: University of New Mexico Press, 1996.

Berry, Wendell. *Home Economics.* New York: North Point Press, 1987.

Blackburn, Thomas C., and Kat Anderson, eds. *Before the Wilderness: Environmental Management by Native Californians.* Menlo Park, CA: Ballena Press, 1993.

Borgmann, Albert. *Crossing the Postmodern Divide.* Chicago: University of Chicago Press, 1993.

Brubaker, Linda. "Vegetation History and Anticipating Future Vegetation Change." In *Ecosystem Management for Parks and Wilderness,* edited by James K. Agee and Darryll R. Johnson, 41–61. Seattle: University of Washington Press, 1988.

Catlin, George. *Letters and Notes on the Manners, Customs, and Conditions of the North American Indians.* Vol. 2. 1841. Reprint, New York: Dover, 1973.

Chase, Alston. *Playing God in Yellowstone: The Destruction of America's First National Park.* San Diego: Harcourt Brace Jovanovich, 1987.

Christensen, Norman L. "Succession and Natural Disturbance: Paradigms, Problems, and Preservation of Natural Ecosystems." In *Ecosystem Management for Parks and Wilderness,* edited by James K. Agee and Darryll R. Johnson, 62–86. Seattle: University of Washington Press, 1988.

Clark, Keith, and Lowell Tiller. *Terrible Trail: The Meek Cutoff, 1845.* Bend, OR: Maverick, 1993.

Cohen, Stan, and Don Miller. *The Big Burn: The Northwest's Forest Fire of 1910.* Missoula, MT: Pictorial Histories, 1978.

Coman, Warren E. "Did the Indian Protect the Forest?" *Pacific Monthly* September 1911, 300–306.

Cowell, C. Mark. "Ecological Restoration and Environmental Ethics." *Environmental Ethics* 15 (Spring 1993): 19–32.

Deckert, E. "Forest Fires in North America: A German View." Translated by George Wetmore Colles. *American Forestry,* May 1911, 273–79.

DeSpelder, Lynne Ann, and Albert Lee Strickland. *The Last Dance: Encountering Death and Dying.* 6th ed. New York: McGraw-Hill Higher Education, 2002.

Devlin, Sherry. "Missoula Foresters Want to Log and Burn the Young to Save the Old." *Missoulian* (Missoula, MT), 22 October 1998.

Dixon, E. James. *Quest for the Origins of the First Americans.* Albuquerque: University of New Mexico Press, 1993.

Dobyns, Henry F. *Their Number Become Thinned: Native American Population Dynamics in Eastern North America.* Knoxville: University of Tennessee Press, 1983.

Doka, Kenneth J., ed. *Disenfranchised Grief: New Directions, Challenges, and Strategies for Practice.* Champaign, IL: Research Press, 2002.

Duke, Cordia Sloan, and Joe B. Frantz. *6,000 Miles of Fence: Life on the XIT Ranch of Texas.* Austin: University of Texas Press, 1961.

Elliot, Robert. "Faking Nature." *Inquiry,* March 1982, 81–93.

Field, Terri. "Caring Relationships with Natural and Artificial Environments." *Environmental Ethics* 17 (Fall 1995): 307–20.

Flores, Dan. *The Natural West: Environmental History in the Great Plains and Rocky Mountains.* Norman: University of Oklahoma Press, 2001.

Freud, Sigmund. *Letters of Sigmund Freud.* Edited by E. L. Freud. Translated by Tania and James Stern. New York: Basic, 1961.

Fussell, E. B. "Idaho's Thirty Days' War." *Collier's Weekly,* 24 September 1910, 16, 26–28.

Graber, David M. "Resolute Biocentrism: The Dilemma of Wilderness in National Parks." In *Reinventing Nature? Responses to Postmodern Deconstruction,* edited by Michael E. Soulé and Gary Lease. Washington, DC: Island Press, 1995.

Gates, Robert J. "Grass Valley Fire Contained." *The Dalles (Ore.) Daily Chronicle,* 13 July 1994.

Greever, Paul R. "Dedication Address—Blackwater Memorial." In the program for the "Dedication Service: Blackwater Firefighters Memorial and Clayton Gulch Marker, Shoshone National Forest, August 20, 1939." U.S. Department of Agriculture, Forest Service.

Griffin, James B. "The Origin and Dispersion of American Indians in North America." In *The First Americans: Origins, Affinities, and Adaptations,* edited by William S. Laughlin and Albert B. Harper, 43–55. New York: Gustav Fischer, 1979.

Gruell, George E. *Fire in Sierra Nevada Forests: A Photographic Interpretation of Ecological Change since 1849.* Missoula, MT: Mountain Press, 2001.

———. "Indian Fires in the Interior West: A Widespread Influence." In *Proceedings—Symposium and Workshop on Wilderness Fire, Missoula,*

Montana, November 15–18, 1983. General Technical Report INT-GTR-182. Ogden, UT: U.S. Department of Agriculture, Forest Service, Intermountain Forest and Range Experiment Station, 1985.

Halm, Joe. "Gallant Joe Halm Tells His Dramatic Experience." *Montana: The Magazine of Western History* 10, no. 4 (1960): 55–58.

Harper, J. Russell. *Paul Kane's Frontier.* Austin: University of Texas Press, 1971.

Hassrick, Peter H. *Frederic Remington: Paintings, Drawings, and Sculpture in the Amon Carter Museum and the Sid W. Richardson Foundation Collections.* New York: Harry N. Abrams, 1973.

Hassrick, Royal B. *The Colorful Story of the American West.* London: Octopus Books, 1975.

———. *The George Catlin Book of American Indians.* New York: Watson-Guptill, 1977.

Higgs, Eric. *Nature by Design: People, Natural Process, and Ecological Restoration.* Cambridge, MA: MIT Press, 2003.

Howe, George E. "The Evolutionary Role of Wildfire in the Northern Rockies and Implications for Resource Managers." In *Proceedings— Tall Timbers Fire Ecology Conference and Fire and Land Management Symposium, No. 14, 8–10 October 1974,* 257–65. Tallahassee: Tall Timbers Research Station, 1976.

Hunn, Eugene S., with James Selam and Family. *Nch'i-Wána: "The Big River": Mid-Columbia Indians and Their Land.* Seattle: University of Washington Press, 1990.

Jansson, Lois. "Have You Ever Stopped to Wonder?" Unpublished autobiography (June 1965). On file with David Turner, public affairs officer, Helena National Forest.

Johnson, Charles G., Jr., Roderick R. Clausnitzer, Peter J. Mehringer, and Chadwick D. Oliver. *Biotic and Abiotic Processes of Eastside Ecosystems: The Effects of Management on Plant and Community Ecology, and on Stand and Landscape Vegetation Dynamics.* General Technical Report PNW-GTR-322. Portland, OR: U.S. Department of Agriculture, Forest Service, Pacific Northwest Research Station, 1994.

Johnson Gottesfeld, Leslie M. "Aboriginal Burning for Vegetation Management in Northwest British Columbia." *Human Ecology*, June 1994, 171–88.

Katz, Eric. "Restoration and Redesign: The Ethical Significance of Human Intervention in Nature." *Restoration and Management Notes* 9 (Winter 1991): 90–96.

Kay, Chales E. "Aboriginal Overkill and Native Burning: Implications for Modern Ecosystem Management." *Western Journal of Applied Forestry* 10, no. 4 (1995): 121–26.

Kierkegaard, Søren. "The Attack upon 'Christendom.'" In *A Kierkegaard Anthology*, edited by Robert Bretall, 448–49. New York: Modern Library, 1946.

Kittredge, William. *The Nature of Generosity.* New York: Alfred A. Knopf, 2000.

Krech, Shepard, III. *The Ecological Indian: Myth and History.* New York: W. W. Norton, 1999.

Kübler-Ross, Elizabeth. *On Death and Dying.* New York: Macmillan, 1969.

Langston, Nancy. *Forest Dreams, Forest Nightmares: The Paradox of Old Growth in the Inland West.* Seattle: University of Washington Press, 1995.

Leopold, Aldo. "Grass, Brush, Timber, and Fire in Southern Arizona." *Journal of Forestry*, October 1924, 1–10.

———. *A Sand County Almanac and Sketches Here and There.* Oxford: Oxford University Press, 1949.

Lewis, Henry T. "Patterns of Indian Burning in California: Ecology and Ethnohistory." In *Before the Wilderness: Environmental Management by Native Californians,* edited by Thomas C. Blackburn and Kat Anderson, 55–116. Menlo Park, CA: Ballena Press, 1993.

———. *A Time for Burning.* Boreal Institute for Northern Studies, Occasional Publication 17. Edmonton: University of Alberta, 1982.

———. "Why Indians Burned: Specific versus General Reasons." In *Proceedings—Symposium and Workshop on Wilderness Fire, Missoula, Montana, November 15–18, 1983.* General Technical Report INT-GTR-182, 75–80. Ogden, UT: U.S. Department of Agriculture, Forest Service, Intermountain Forest and Range Experiment Station, 1985.

Lewis, Meriwether. Journal entry for "Friday July 19th 1805." In *April 7–July 27, 1805.* Vol. 4 of *The Journals of the Lewis and Clark Expedition,* edited by Gary E. Moulton, 402–405. Lincoln: University of Nebraska Press, 1987.

Lorbiecki, Marybeth. *Aldo Leopold: A Fierce Green Fire.* Helena, MT: Falcon, 1996.

Maclean, Norman. *Young Men and Fire.* Chicago: University of Chicago Press, 1992.

Malouf, Carling I. "Flathead and Pend d'Oreille." In *Plateau,* edited by Deward E. Walker Jr., 297–326. Vol. 12 of *Handbook of North American Indians,* edited by William C. Sturtevant. Washington, DC: Smithsonian Institution, 1998.

Manning, Richard. "The Failure of Literature." In *Northern Lights: A Selection of New Writing from the American West,* edited by Deborah Clow and Donald Snow, 67–75. New York: Vintage Books, 1994.

Marshall, Robert. "Mountain Ablaze." *Nature,* June–July 1953, Forest Service Reprint, 4. Quoted in Stephen J. Pyne, *Fire in America: A Cultural History of Wildland and Rural Fire* (Princeton, NJ: Princeton University Press, 1988), 188.

Martinez, Dennis. "Indigenous Patterns of Burning." Paper presented at the annual meeting of the Society for Ecological Restoration, Austin, Tex., September 1998.

Matsch, Charles L. *North America and the Great Ice Age.* New York: Mc-Graw-Hill, 1976.

McCracken, Harold. *George Catlin and the Old Frontier.* New York: Bonanza Books, 1959.

Mehringer, Peter J., Jr., Stephen F. Arno, and Kenneth L. Petersen. "Postglacial History of Lost Trail Pass Bog, Bitterroot Mountains, Montana." *Arctic and Alpine Research* 9, no. 4 (1977): 345–68.

Meine, Curt. *Aldo Leopold: His Life and Work.* Madison: University of Wisconsin Press, 1988.

Meyers, Barbara. "Disenfranchised Grief and the Loss of an Animal Companion." In *Disenfranchised Grief: New Directions, Challenges, and Strategies for Practice,* edited by Kenneth J. Doka, 251–64. Champaign, IL: Research Press, 2002.

[U.S. Forest Service document.] *Montana: The Magazine of Western History* 10, no. 3 (1960): 58.

National Wildfire Coordinating Group. *Historical Wildland Fire-fighter Fatalities, 1910–1996.* 2d ed. PMS 822/NFES 1849. N.p.: U.S. Department of Agriculture, U.S. Department of the Interior, and the National Association of State Foresters, 1997.

Norton, Bryan G. *Toward Unity among Environmentalists.* New York: Oxford University Press, 1991.

Perrine, Laurence. *Literature: Structure, Sound, and Sense.* 4th ed. New York: Harcourt Brace Jovanovich, 1983.

Point, Nicolas. *Wilderness Kingdom: Indian Life in the Rocky Mountains: 1840–1847, The Journals and Paintings of Nicolas Point, S.J.* Trans. Joseph P. Donnelly. Chicago: Loyola University Press, 1967.

Powell, John Wesley. *Report on the Lands of the Arid Region of the United States, With a More Detailed Account of the Lands of Utah.* 2d ed. Washington, DC: Government Printing Office, 1879.

Pratt, John Lowell, ed. *Currier & Ives: Chronicles of America.* Maplewood, NJ: Hammond, 1968.

Pulaski, Edward C. "Surrounded by Forest Fires: My Most Exciting Experience as a Forest Ranger." *American Forestry,* August 1923, 485–86.

Pyne, Stephen J. *Burning Bush: A Fire History of Australia.* New York: Henry Holt, 1991.

———. *Fire in America: A Cultural History of Wildland and Rural Fire.* Princeton, NJ: Princeton University Press, 1988.

———. *World Fire: The Culture of Fire on Earth.* New York: Henry Holt, 1995.

Rando, Therese A. *Grieving: How to Go On Living When Someone You Love Dies.* Lexington, MA: Lexington Books, 1988.

Racicot, Marc. To the Editor. *Glenwood (Colo.) Post,* 7 July 1995.

"Random Talk on Forest Fires." *American Forestry,* November 1910, 667–69.

Robbins, William G., and Donald W. Wolf. *Landscape and the Intermontane Northwest: An Environmental History.* General Technical Report PNW-GTR-319. Portland, OR: U.S. Department of Agriculture, Forest Service, Pacific Northwest Research Station, 1994.

Rolston, Holmes. "Valuing Wildlands." *Environmental Ethics* 7, no. 1 (1985): 23–48.

Romme, William H., and Don G. Despain. "Historical Perspective on the Yellowstone Fires of 1988: A Reconstruction of Prehistoric Fire History Reveals That Comparable Fires Occurred in the Early 1700s." *Bioscience* 39, no.10 (1989): 695–99.

————. "The Long History of Fire in the Greater Yellowstone Ecosystem." *Western Wildlands* 15 (Summer 1989): 10–17.

Ross, Marvin C. *The West of Alfred Jacob Miller.* Norman: University of Oklahoma Press, 1968.

Saul, Darin Allen. "Restoring Culture and Nature: Land Use Ecology in the Palouse River Watershed." Ph.D. diss., Washington State University, 1996.

Schaner, Michelle. "Storm King, Three Years Later: A Day to Remember, a Day to Pay Tribute." *Glenwood (Colo.) Post,* 7 July 1997.

Shinn, Dean A. "Historical Perspectives on Range Burning in the Inland Pacific Northwest." *Journal of Range Management,* 33, no. 6 (1980): 415–23.

Silcox, F. A. "How the Fires Were Fought." *American Forestry,* November 1910, 631–39.

Snyder, Gary. "The Place, the Region, and the Commons." In *Environmental Philosophy: From Animal Rights to Radical Ecology,* edited by Michael E. Zimmerman et al., 441–56. 2d ed. Upper Saddle River, NJ: Prentice Hall, 1998.

Soulé, Michael E. "The Social Siege of Nature." In *Reinventing Nature? Responses to Postmodern Deconstruction,* edited by Michael E. Soulé and Gary Lease, 137–70. Washington, DC: Island Press, 1995.

Soulé, Michael E., and Gary Lease, eds. *Reinventing Nature? Responses to Postmodern Deconstruction.* Washington, DC: Island Press, 1995.

Stewart, Omar C. "Fire as the First Great Force Employed by Man." In *Man's Role in Changing the Face of the Earth,* ed. William L. Thomas, 115–33. Chicago: University of Chicago Press, 1956.

Strohmaier, David J. *The Seasons of Fire: Reflections on Fire in the West.* Reno: University of Nevada Press, 2001.

———. "Threescore and Ten: Fire, Place, and Loss in the West." *Ethics & the Environment* 8, no. 2 (Fall 2003): 31–41.

Thoreau, Henry David. "Life without Principle." In *The Major Essays of Henry David Thoreau,* edited by Richard Dillman, 113–30. Albany, NY: Whitston, 2001.

Toole, David. *Waiting for Godot in Sarajevo: Theological Reflections on Nihilism, Tragedy, and Apocalypse.* Boulder, CO: Westview Press, 1998.

Turner, David. *The Thirteenth Fire: The Story of Montana's Mann Gulch Fire.* Helena, MT: U.S. Department of Agriculture, Forest Service, Helena National Forest, 1999.

U.S. Department of the Interior, Bureau of Land Management. *1961 Fire Plan for the Prineville Grazing District.* Prineville, OR: U.S. Department of the Interior, Bureau of Land Management, Prineville District, ca. 1961.

Vale, Thomas R. "The Myth of the Humanized Landscape: An Example from Yosemite National Park." *Natural Areas Journal* 18, no. 3 (1998): 231–35.

Weltzien, O. Alan. "Norman Maclean and Laird Robinson: A Tale of Two Research Partners." *Montana: The Magazine of Western History* 45, no. 1 (1995): 46–55.

———."The Two Lives of Norman Maclean and the Text of Fire in *Young Men and Fire.*" *Western American Literature* 29, no. 1 (1994): 3–24.

Williams, Gerald W. "American Indian Use of Fire in Ecosystems: Thousands of Years of Managing Landscapes." Revision of a paper presented at the annual meeting of the American Ecological Society, Albuquerque, August 1997. Portland, OR: U.S. Department of Agriculture, Forest Service, Pacific Northwest Region, 1997. Photocopy.

———. "References on the American Indian Use of Fire in Ecosystems." Portland, OR: U.S. Department of Agriculture, Forest Service, Pacific Northwest Region, 1997. Photocopy.

Williams, Michael. *Americans and Their Forests: A Historical Geography.* New York: Cambridge University Press, 1989.

Wilson, Edward O. *Biophilia.* Cambridge, MA: Harvard University Press, 1984.

Worden, William J. *Grief Counseling and Grief Therapy: A Handbook for the Mental Health Practitioner.* 2d ed. New York: Springer, 1991.

Worster, Donald. *Nature's Economy: A History of Ecological Ideas.* 2d ed. New York: Cambridge University Press, 1994.

INDEX